ESPN Ultimate Highlight Reel

ESPN *Ultimate Highlight Reel*

The 365 Wildest, Weirdest, Most Unforgettable
SportsCenter Moments of All Time

ESPN BOOKS   MELCHER MEDIA

"A ... Picture ... Is ... Worth ... A ... Thousand ... Words."

By Chris Berman

Long before ESPN was born, in 1979, and I was hired as an unknown and very wet-behind-the-ears aspiring TV sportscaster at the tender age of 24, I subscribed to that adage.

Little did I know that such an old saying would become the unspoken hallmark—the genius, really—of the network that we have all enjoyed for close to three decades now.

Think I'm kidding? Just flip on *SportsCenter* tonight.

What you'll see is a turbocharged highlight reel of the best and the biggest stuff that's taken place that day in the world of sports—*your* world. (And *mine.*)

Think about it. If there are 15 major league baseball games played on a sunny Sunday afternoon in September, *and* 14 NFL games, *and* a golf tournament or two, *and* a NASCAR race, *and* a big X sports competition going on ... Or if on a frosty fall Saturday there's a full lineup of college football games *and* NHL games *and* more college football games ...

How many different competitions is that, each with its own turning points and big plays? How could we possibly tell you what happened in even one day of sports with words alone? But because *A ... PICTURE ... IS ... WORTH ... A ... THOUSAND ... WORDS ...*

Well, you get the picture, don't you?

The presentation of highlights has been the backbone of ESPN from our very start in 1979.

Every contest, no matter how "big" or "small," is its own mini drama. Each begins with a blank canvas. In each, somebody wins and somebody loses, somebody steps up to make the big catch or smash the big hit—sometimes according to expectations, more often not. It's our job to *show you* the who, the what, and the why of the wins and losses that make your world—and ours—go around.

It's not easy to boil down a three-hour game into a nice, neat, 45-second bite that shows you the essence of what happened. Not easy, but it's our labor of love here at ESPN, because we're genuinely excited every day by the challenge of showing you what we saw.

Hey, you'd do the same for us, right? That's because sports fans always want to talk sports with sports fans. And that's the way we see our highlights: as a really big sports fan in Bristol, Connecticut, reaching out to an equally big sports fan in ... Seattle, Washington, or Pensacola, Florida, or Bangor, Maine, or Rapid City, South Dakota.

Our job—and who could ask for a better one?—is to deliver information with respect, accuracy, and excitement while you look at the pictures. In other words, to narrate what you're seeing as if we were talking to a friend. (Which, of course, we are.) Now, my personal approach—that is, my decibel level and penchant for having fun with what we're seeing together—might be different from another anchor's approach. Doesn't matter. Doesn't mean one's better than the other. All that matters is that we communicate our passion for the sports we're highlighting for you.

As a fan, I want to *see* a key play happen. I don't want to be told what's going to happen by somebody who already knows. All of us in front of the camera are pretty sure you feel the same way.

So the First Commandment of delivering highlights is simple: Do it as if they were happening live. Sure, I've already seen them, and I know what's going to happen next, but most of the time you don't, so why should I spoil the fun?

That's why I'll never say, "Tom Brady hit Deion Branch for a 50-yard touchdown," *until he does it.*

And I'll never say, "Derek Jeter doubles off the wall," *until the ball hits the wall.*

My own personal favorite highlights through the years? Don't get me started! It's impossible to say. Look at the math: G (for Games) x P (for Pictures) x 27 Years (and counting) = ... ???

But I'll try.

Let's see, Cal Ripken running around Camden Yards the night he broke Lou Gehrig's consecutive-games streak ... Joe Montana to Dwight Clark for The Catch ... Magic Johnson's little jump-sky hook in those classic Lakers-Celtics Finals ... Guy Lafleur flying down the wing and scoring on a cannonading blast ... Payne Stewart winning the U.S. Open with a 15-foot putt on the 72nd hole ... Phil Mickelson doing the same thing at the Masters ... Brett Favre scrambling and firing a long touchdown pass ... Adam Vinatieri's 45-yard-long field goal through the snow in the playoffs ... Junior Griffey rounding third on Edgar Martinez's hit to score the winning run in the playoffs against the Yankees ...

Stop!

Like I said, you shouldn't have gotten me started. Undoubtedly, you have your own list of all-time favorite highlights—and I'm betting some of them will turn up in the pages of the book you're holding right now. The tricks of the calendar have given us a bigger bounty of highlights on some days, but between these covers are a full year's worth of super highlights. Hey, maybe you'll even find some new personal favorites.

So kick back, relax, and enjoy *ESPN Ultimate Highlight Reel*. If you have half as much fun reading it as we did pulling it together, you're in for a great ride.

And remember, you already know how much a picture is worth, so seeing *is* believing.

January

Unwelcome Wagon

January 1, 1985
Sooner Schooner

Late in the third quarter of the Orange Bowl, the Oklahoma Sooners recovered a Washington Huskies fumble and drove the ball down the field, where Tim Lashar kicked a 22-yard field goal to put them up 17-14. Just as the players were beginning to realize that Oklahoma had been flagged for illegal procedure, the Sooner Schooner—the covered wagon that's the treasured symbol for school, team, and state—charged onto the field to celebrate the score. The wagon almost hit several players and the refs tacked on another 15 yards for unsportsmanlike conduct. Lashar's now-42-yard attempt was blocked. Oklahoma went on to lose the game 28-17, and with it any hopes the Sooners had for the national championship.

Guts Play

January 2, 1984
Nebraska vs. Miami

What's it take to make an entire state scream "Kick!" all at once? Try heavily favored Nebraska's rejecting a tie and going for the two-point conversion to win the Orange Bowl and the national championship. The Huskers had come back from being two TDs down even after their Heisman-winning RB Mike Rozier was sidelined in the third quarter. With 48 seconds left in the game after a touchdown and still down by a point, coach Tom Osborne never flinched. "We wanted an undefeated season and the national championship," said Osborne. QB Turner Gill rolled out, saw Jeff Smith open, and fired away. Miami defensive back Ken Calhoun batted the toss away and the Hurricanes kicked off their dynasty with a 31-30 win.

Lion in Winter

January 2, 1987
Pete Giftopoulos

It was billed by the press as crass against class, evil vs. good. The swaggering Miami Hurricanes arrived in Arizona for the Fiesta Bowl wearing combat fatigues; the gentlemanly Penn State Nittany Lions arrived in jackets and ties. Penn State seemed way outgunned—and indeed, they would be outgained, 162 yards to Miami's 445. But a string of turnovers had given the Nittany Lions a late-in-the-game 14-10 lead. Vinny Testaverde was moving the Canes toward a storybook finish, but with nine seconds left in the game, Penn State LB Pete Giftopoulos tracked a Testaverde throw like he'd read Vinny's mind, and made the pick at the Penn State one. A few ticks later, a youthful Joe Paterno was being carried by a pride of Nittany Lions.

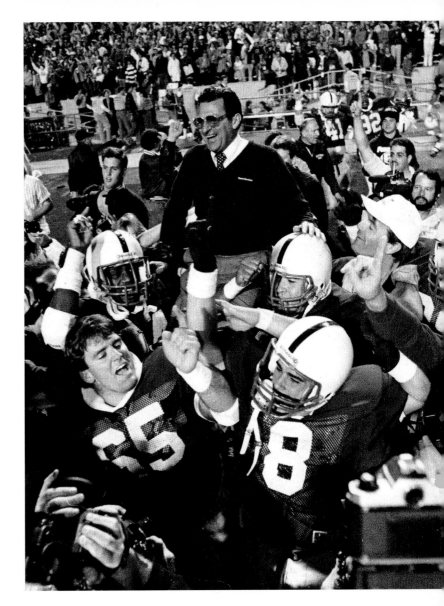

Leaking Oilers

January 3, 1993
Frank Reich

As a Maryland Terrapin, Frank Reich was a backup
QB who led the biggest comeback in NCAA history (*see*
November 10, 1984). As a Buffalo Bill, he was a clipboard
guy—the guy in the baseball hat who showed up in case
future Hall of Famer Jim Kelly got hit by a bus in the
parking lot prior to the game. On this day, Reich started
the wild-card playoff game for the injured Kelly, and in the
third quarter, his Bills trailed the Oilers 35-3. The Oilers
had no idea they should be nervous—but Reich had them
right where he wanted them. In less than seven minutes,
the Bills scored four touchdowns to get close, and then,
late in the fourth quarter, Reich hit Andre Reed for the
receiver's third TD of the day and the Bills pulled ahead.
Houston managed to tie the game with a field goal and
send it into overtime, but Warren Moon was picked again
at his 37, and a face-masking call on the return put the
Bills close enough for the winning chip shot. Reich's line
for the day: 21-34, 289, 4 TDs. Final score: Buffalo 41,
Houston 38.

Tough Nuts to Crack

January 3, 2003
Miami vs. Ohio State

In the second overtime of the national championship game at the Fiesta Bowl, Ohio State's Maurice Clarett powered his way into the end zone to put the Buckeyes up 31-24. But the drama wasn't over. When Miami got the ball, QB Ken Dorsey was sent to the sideline with a minor injury. Backup Derrick Crudup hit an eight-yard pass to set up a fourth and three. Back in came Dorsey, who earned a big first down. A few plays later, now facing fourth and goal, he dropped back and chucked a desperate pass, and OSU crusher Matt Wilhelm swatted the ball to the ground. For the first time in 34 years, the Buckeyes were national champions.

Somewhere, John Heisman Was Smiling

January 4, 2005
Oklahoma vs. USC

With the national championship on the line at the Orange Bowl, Matt Leinart, the tall, left-handed Southern Cal quarterback with a Heisman Trophy already resting on his bookcase, faced an Oklahoma defense that hadn't given up a TD in its previous three games. How was he? Only amazing. The first of Leinart's four first-half touchdown strikes was to tight end Dominique Byrd, who made a spectacular one-handed snag to tie the game 7-7. Early in the second quarter, now with a 14-7 lead, Leinart hit Dwayne Jarrett for this 54-yard score. Less than three minutes later, Leinart hooked up with Steve Smith for a five-yard TD. For good measure, with 1:56 left in the half, he hit Smith again for six from 33 yards. Oklahoma hadn't witnessed so much devastation since the Dust Bowl. Leinart coasted in the second half: only one TD pass. Final score? USC 55, Oklahoma 19. MVP? Three guesses.

Best Game of All Time?

January 4, 2006
Vince Young

A Rose Bowl showdown between two undefeated, dominant teams, with a huddle's worth of All-Americas (past, current, future) on the field, playing for the national championship, in the most storied football stadium in the land. Any wonder that Texas-USC turned out to be a pretty good game? Texas spoiled USC's bid for a third consecutive national title, 41-38, largely because of a Vince Young performance for the ages. In less than seven minutes at the end of the game, Young led two TD drives to rally his team from a 12-point deficit, scoring both touchdowns himself—the second on fourth and five from the 8 with just 19 seconds left to play.

Big Whack Attack

January 6, 1994
Nancy Kerrigan

After practicing for the U.S. Figure Skating Championships, Olympic gold medal hopeful Nancy Kerrigan was assaulted by a police-baton-swinging thug—hired by competitor Tonya Harding's now ex-husband and a friend—who bashed the skater's right knee. "Why me?" screamed Kerrigan after she was attacked. The obvious answer: she was probably going to kick Harding's butt on the ice.

Music City Marvel

January 8, 2000
Kevin Dyson

It was a wild-card game, and it certainly was wild. In the last two minutes, each team thought they'd won it: Tennessee when they kicked a field goal with 1:48 left for a 15-13 lead; Buffalo after Steve Christie punched a FG through with 16 seconds left to put the Bills up 16-15. Then, on the ensuing kickoff, Christie shanked a pop-up that was fielded by Titans fullback Lorenzo Neal at the 25, and the fun began. Neal promptly handed the ball to TE Frank Wycheck, who ran right, spun, and fired the ball across the field to WR Kevin Dyson, who grabbed the ball just before it hit the ground and took off down the sideline behind a wall of beef. And yes, he did ... Go! ... All! ... The! ... Way! The play was reviewed to make sure Wycheck's lateral wasn't a forward pass, but the ruling on the field stood. Final score: 22-16.

The Catch

January 10, 1982
Joe Montana to Dwight Clark

The 49ers had driven 83 yards to the Cowboys'
6, and 58 seconds remained in the NFC
Championship. Joe Montana wasn't a legend
yet, but he would become one on the next
snap. The former Notre Dame QB rolled to his
right, looked for Freddie Solomon, then caught
a glimpse of Dwight Clark in the back of the
end zone. Off the wrong foot, Montana fluttered
a high, soft ball toward Clark, who snatched
it from the sky and thrust his team into its
first Super Bowl. The extra point made it San
Francisco 28, Dallas 27—and a dynasty was
on the move. "The play was nothing special,"
said San Francisco coach Bill Walsh afterward.
"We worked on it from the first day of camp."
To this day, San Fran fans—and Cowboys fans,
even more so—beg to differ.

The Drive

January 11, 1987
John Elway

The Cleveland defense had been unyielding most of the day, and with 5:43 left on the clock, the Browns held a 20-13 lead—and the Denver offense pinned down on their own 2. No wonder the Dawg Pound faithful were in full bark: a trip to the Super Bowl was on the line. Broncos QB John Elway assessed the situation the same way every football player has since pigs first sacrificed their bladders in the name of sport: "We just had to dig down and find out what we were made of." And Elway found something. Facing second and seven at his 15, Elway was chased from the pocket and picked up 11 yards on a gimpy ankle. But the biggest of many big plays came on third and 18 at the Cleveland 43, when Elway found Mark Jackson for 20 yards and the first down. A few plays later, he hit Jackson for the score that tied the game at 20-20. Denver went on to win 23-20 on a Rich Karlis field goal in OT. "We worked on containing Elway all week, and we did, until the very end," lamented Cleveland coach Marty Schottenheimer in a somber Browns locker room.

This Eagle Can Fly

January 11, 2004
Donovan McNabb to Freddie Mitchell

Trying to make it to a third consecutive NFC
Championship game, the Eagles were looking more
like doves. They were down by three and faced fourth
and 26 from their own 26 with just over a minute left
in the game. The Packers secondary went into their
Prevent D—but something happened on their way to
prevention. Philly wideout Freddie Mitchell found a
seam, and Donovan McNabb, running for his life, hit
him for a 28-yard gain. A few plays later, Philly kicker
David Akers knotted the game at 17-17 and sent it into
overtime, where he won it with another field goal after
Brian Dawkins picked off a Brett Favre pass.

Ex-Hail Mary

January 14, 1996
Steelers vs. Colts

Bill Cowher's Steelers had been among the AFC's best all season long, but as they nursed a 20-16 lead with 1:34 left in the conference championship game, Pittsburgh fans got a little worried. Indianapolis QB Jim Harbaugh marched his Colts from their own 16 to the Steelers' 29 while somehow managing to keep five ticks on the clock—just enough time to loft the most tantalizing Hail Mary toss in playoff history. As the ball floated into a throng of players jostling in the end zone, it was initially tipped by Steelers safety Darren Perry. Then the ball was nicked by Willie Williams, another Steelers DB. Then it hit Colts wideout Aaron Bailey in the chest as he was falling to the ground. He reached for it. The ball rolled down his stomach! He strained for it. The ball rolled down to his thigh! But he couldn't get a handle on it and Pittsburgh DB Randy Fuller swatted it away. The next day, everybody in Pittsburgh swore they knew they had the game locked up all the way.

Big Tackle for Big Ben

January 15, 2006
Ben Roethlisberger

What is it with the Steelers and the Colts in January? Ten years plus one day after the Ex-Hail Mary game (*see* January 14, 1996), and with his team leading the Colts 21-18 in an AFC divisional playoff game, Pittsburgh's Ben Roethlisberger handed off to Jerome Bettis on the Indy 2-yard line for what seemed like a certain TD. Instead, The Bus had a head-on collision with defenders and coughed up the rock, which was scooped up by Colts' DB Nick Harper, who appeared to have nothing but synthetic turf between him and a 98-yard go-ahead score. But Big Ben had begun backpedaling toward midfield as soon as he saw the ball squirt loose, and now he lunged at Harper's ankles and brought him down on the Colts' 42 with a game-saving tackle. Peyton Manning took his team down to the Steelers' 28 with 21 seconds left, where Mike Vanderjagt, one of the NFL's best kickers, missed a field goal that would have sent the game into OT. Ring up the win to Big Ben's outstanding D.

Snatch and Grab

January 16, 2005
L.J. Smith to Freddie Mitchell

A year after his startling fourth-and-26 catch in a division playoff against the Packers (*see* January 11, 2004), Freddie Mitchell did it again, this time in a division playoff game against the Vikings. With the Eagles up 14-7 over Minnesota but struggling to widen the gap, Donovan McNabb hit tight end L.J. Smith inside the Vikings' 10. As he rumbled toward the goal line, Smith was knocked into a 360° orbit and the ball spurted high into the air—right into the hands of Mitchell, who was in the end zone. Said Mitchell after the game, which sent the Eagles to a fourth straight NFC Championship matchup: "I just want to thank my hands for being so great."

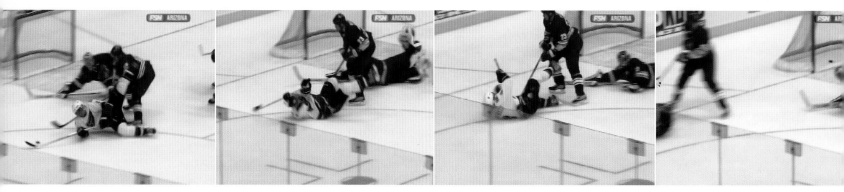

Even The Great One Was Amazed

January 16, 2006
Alexander Ovechkin

One thing about coaching hockey versus playing it—you get a ringside seat for all the action. Just ask Phoenix coach Wayne Gretzky for his take on the second goal Capitals winger Alex Ovechkin scored in a 6-1 Washington rout of the Coyotes. Completely sprawled out on the ice and sliding toward the corner, Ovechkin rolled from his back to his chest and reached out with his stick to poke the puck into the net. Said coach Great One afterward, "That was pretty sweet." He should know.

Déjà vu All Over Again

January 17, 1988
Earnest Byner

In the AFC Championship game a year earlier against the Browns, John Elway led the Broncos the length of the field to force the game into OT and Denver went on to win on a field goal (*see January 11, 1987*). This time, Denver held the lead and Cleveland had the length of the field to cover to tie the game. Starting from his own 25 with 3:53 left to play, QB Bernie Kosar confidently maneuvered the Browns toward sweet revenge. When Kosar handed off to Earnest Byner at the Denver 8, the big back tucked the ball as he braced for a collision with a pair of Broncos DBs, Jeremiah Castille and Tony Lilly. Next thing anyone knew, the ball was on the ground with Castille on top of it. "I tried to split two guys," said Byner, "and the ball just popped out." Also popped? The sanity of Cleveland fans, who for the second straight year suffered an agonizing final-seconds loss to Denver in the championship game.

On Second Thought ...

January 19, 2002
Tom Brady

Fumble! That's what everyone saw and that's what referee Walt Coleman called it when Oakland's Charles Woodson knocked the ball from Tom Brady's hands. And so, with the Raiders in possession and leading 13-10 with 1:43 left to play, the game was all but over. But hold on—there was less than two minutes remaining so the play had to be reviewed. To the shock of everyone, it was overturned. *Incomplete pass!* "His hand was coming forward, which makes it an incomplete pass," Coleman explained later. "He has to get it all the way tucked back in order for it to be a fumble." On the next play, Brady completed a 13-yard pass to David Patten. Four plays later, a low 45-yard field goal tied the score at 13-13 with 27 seconds left. The Pats won 16-13 on a 23-yard Adam Vinatieri field goal in OT.

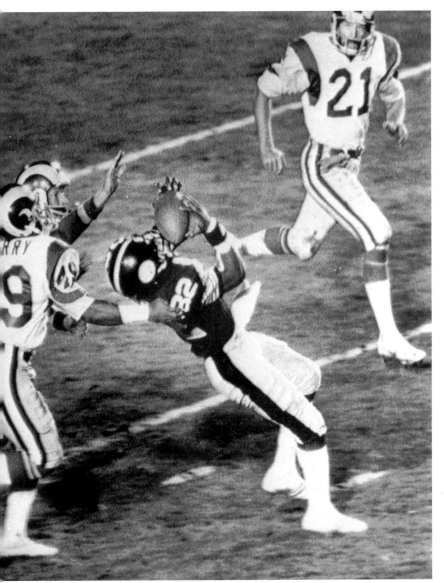

Steeling One

January 20, 1980
Terry Bradshaw to John Stallworth

The Steelers dynasty was looking for its fourth Super Bowl win in six years. The Rams ... well, they weren't really supposed to be much of a match for Pittsburgh. With the clock creeping toward 12:00 left in the game, however, the Rams stubbornly clung to a 19-17 lead and the Steelers appeared discombobulated as they faced third and eight from their own 27. Steelers WR John Stallworth lined up to run a short hook pattern, but noticed that the Rams defense was misaligned. He did hook, but then took off and kept running ... and running. Terry Bradshaw uncorked a bomb and Stallworth managed to catch it in traffic. The 73-yard play gave the Steelers a 24-19 lead. They scored again later to make the final 31-19, but the play that gave the Steelers ring No. 4 was Stallworth's hook-and-run-run-run.

Fire Down Under

January 21, 1990
John McEnroe

Johnny Mac hadn't won a major tournament since the 1984 U.S. Open, but he arrived in Sydney for the Australian Open with his game intact. He played cagey, effective tennis to move into the fourth round, where he faced Mikael Pernfors. Despite being in control of the match most of the way, McEnroe's legendary temper finally accomplished the one thing it had always failed to do—it got its owner thrown completely out of the tournament. After an endless tirade that included high-decibel expletives and vulgarities, coupled with a thrown racquet, McEnroe finally got tossed while leading 6-1, 4-6, 7-5, 2-4. At one point, McEnroe was enraged by a crying baby and hollered into the stands, "Give him a drink, the boy's hungry." After the umpire asked the parents to remove the child, a fan yelled out, "Can we breathe, John?"

Kobe Brings the Beef

January 22, 2006
Kobe Bryant

Hitting 28 of his 46 shots from the field and 18 of his 20 free throws, Kobe Bryant hung 81 points on Toronto in a Lakers-Raptors game at the Staples Center. Michael Jordan never scored that many in a game (69 was his best), nor did Kareem Abdul-Jabbar, the league's all-time leading scorer, who never threw down more than 55. Only Wilt Chamberlain had scored more in one game (100 on 36 of 63 from the field, 28 of 32 from the line; *see* March 2, 1962), making Bryant's performance deadly efficient by comparison. "Eighty-one is 81," said admiring peer Vince Carter of the Nets. "I don't care if you're playing summer league, pickup, or PlayStation."

Sometimes It Only Takes One Play

January 23, 2000
Kurt Warner to Ricky Proehl

It was the NFC Championship, but the score—Buccaneers 6, Rams 5—seemed like something from a diamond in the eighth inning, not a gridiron in the fourth quarter. Tampa Bay's ferocious D had stifled St. Louis' "Greatest Show on Turf" offense all day. Then, with 4:44 left in the game, Bucs defenders brought on the heat. Rams QB Kurt Warner saw the blitz coming and lobbed a deep ball to the end zone in the direction of wideout Ricky Proehl, who hadn't caught a touchdown pass all year. This time, though, Proehl out-jumped Tampa Bay DB Brian Kelly and came down with a trip to the Super Bowl. "Nobody had stopped them like we did," said Bucs safety John Lynch, who arrived at the scene a split second too late. "That's all it takes sometimes—one play and you lose." Final score: 11-6. Funny, it still sounds like a baseball game.

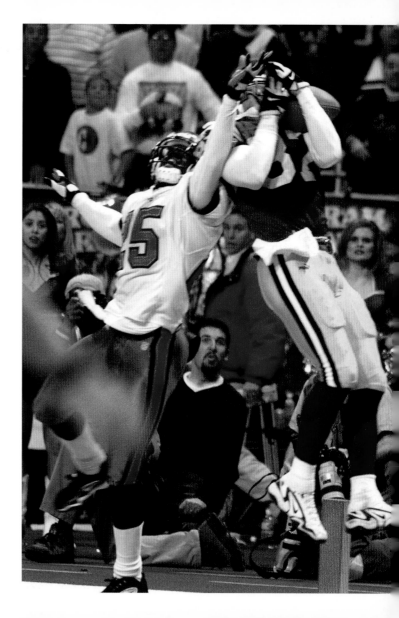

Standup Job

January 24, 1982
49ers vs. Bengals

With the third quarter nearing its end, the 20-7 lead San Francisco had over Cincinnati in Super Bowl XVI looked like it was about to be cut in half. The Bengals were sitting on first and goal at the 49ers 3, and no less a true believer than Niners linebacker Jack "Hacksaw" Reynolds said later, "I really didn't think we could stop them." First Cincy's 249-pound fullback/battering ram Pete Johnson crashed to the 1 on first down. Johnson got the call again on second but was hit high by Reynolds and low by rookie tackle John Harty: no gain. Thinking the Niners D would be lying in wait for Johnson on third, Ken Anderson flipped a short pass to his other back, Charles Alexander, but linebacker Dan Bunz stopped him cold: no gain. On fourth down, it was Johnson's turn again. "Johnson's like a Sherman tank," Reynolds said. "He goes to a hole and I go to fill the hole. I really don't remember what I did on that play." What he did was smash into Johnson at the same time that Ronnie Lott did: no gain. "I don't know what part of Pete I had," said the rookie Lott. "I had something, and I was just going to hold on. Pete is a powerful man. He's hard to bring down." But not impossible. Final score: 49ers 26, Bengals 21.

Break Point

January 25, 1988
Jerome Lane

It wasn't bad enough that Pitt whomped on Providence 90-56 in a Big East blowout. And it wasn't bad enough that the Panthers' Jerome Lane chalked up 17 points and 17 boards. But when he scored two of those points on a sky-high tomahawk dunk, tore loose the rim, and exploded the backboard, raining Plexiglas and ignominy down on the Friars in equal measure, that was just plain *baaad!* Badder still, it gave the guys on *SportsCenter* the classic line: "Send it in, Jerome!"

Fourth Time's the Charm

January 25, 1998
John Elway

After three losing trips to the Super Bowl, John Elway wasn't going to let gimpy knees and a 37-year-old body stand between him and a ring. With the Broncos facing third and six in the third quarter at the Packers' 12, Elway ran from the pocket and headed toward the first-down marker. He knew he was going to have to leap for this one, and when he did, he got 360ed by three Green Bay defenders. But when he landed, it was first and goal. Elway shot up from the ground, pumped his fist, and led the Broncos the rest of the way to a 31-24 win and their first Super Bowl rings.

Cool Running

January 26, 1986
William Perry

Trailing the Bears 37-3 in the third quarter of Super Bowl XX, the Patriots must have figured nothing much else could go wrong. But a big—really big—part of the best defense in history was about to rub their noses in it. Chicago's William "Refrigerator" Perry, 6'2" and 308 pounds worth of talented defensive lineman—back when 308 pounds meant something—entered the game on first and goal at the New England 1. "I thought I was going in to block for Walter," said Perry. "But coach Ditka told me to tell Jim to call 'H-44, dive left.' I carry the ball on that play. I was excited. I just ran behind Jimbo Covert. I didn't know it would be that easy." Perry scored practically untouched and gave the ball a spike as if he'd been scoring TDs his whole life. Fellow RB Walter Payton was merely a decoy.

Sacre Bleu!

January 27, 1995
Eric Cantona

Manchester United's star striker, Eric Cantona, had some anger management issues. He once punched his own goalie in the face, and on another occasion kicked a ball into the crowd and threw his shirt at the referee. When a fan at a Man United-Crystal Palace game threw something at him and shouted what Cantona, a Frenchman, claimed were racial insults, he didn't kick the ball into the crowd—he kicked the fan. As far as assaults on fans go, this was a beauty: Cantona landed both feet on the man's chest in a classic kung-fu kick, then proceeded to pummel him. Two days later, Cantona faced some management anger issues in the form of a fine reported to be £20,000, a nine-month suspension, and his removal as captain of the French national team.

Picking a Winner

January 28, 1996
Larry Brown

Barry Switzer's Cowboys were hanging on by the skin of their stars, cradling a three-point lead over the Steelers with 4:15 left in Super Bowl XXX. Pittsburgh had been avoiding Deion Sanders all day, instead trying to pick on his D-mate at the other Dallas corner, Larry Brown. Earlier in the game, Brown had made a pick that set up a touchdown, and just now, as the Steelers were driving for the possible go-ahead score, he let instinct take over. When the Boys blitzed, Brown sensed Neil O'Donnell would throw a quick slant, so he jumped on it. In fact, he jumped on it much better than intended receiver Andre Hastings, who slanted the wrong way and wound up a country mile from the ball, which went right to Brown, who went right to the 6-yard line. Two plays later, it was Dallas 27, Pittsburgh 17, and that's the way it stayed. Explained game MVP Brown afterward, "I was on the same page with the quarterback. The receiver was off the page."

Losing His Grip

January 29, 2005
Chuck Carothers

With his patented Carolla trick (*see* August 5, 2004), which involved a 360, a barrel roll, and sometimes the kitchen sink, X Games moto X gold medalist Chuck Carothers was the heavy favorite at Winter X Nine. Instead, Carothers ended up taking a tire to the gut and finishing dead last. As his bike headed toward the ground on his second attempt, he lost his grip on the handlebars and crashed on top of the right tire. "I had to go for it," he said later, explaining, quite accurately, "The only person who can beat me is myself."

Short Yardage

January 30, 2000
Rams vs. Titans

With 22 seconds remaining in Super Bowl XXXIV and his team trailing 23-16, Titans QB Steve McNair was on the run. After taking the snap at the Rams' 26, he physically repulsed two sack attempts while dropping back to the 36, where he let rip a pass to Kevin Dyson, who took it to the 10. Tennessee spent its final time out with six seconds left and settled on a play that used tight end Frank Wycheck as a ruse to allow Dyson to run a quick slant. McNair nailed Dyson inside the 5, and the receiver turned upfield for pay dirt. He almost got there, but St. Louis linebacker Mike Jones dragged him to the ground on the 1-yard line as the clock expired. "It seemed like slow motion," Jones said. "I couldn't see McNair throw the ball, but I could feel it." For Dyson, who'd scored the Music City Miracle TD (*see January 8, 2000*), it probably didn't seem slow enough.

Lett-ing It Slip Away

January 31, 1993
Leon Lett vs. Don Beebe

The Cowboys had Super Bowl XXVII tucked safely away in the fourth quarter when 6'6", 292-pound defensive tackle Leon Lett scooped up a fumble by the Bills' Frank Reich at the Dallas 35. The right side of the field was wide open and Lett started rumbling toward the end zone. This was the stuff linemen's dreams are made of; Lett said later that it would have been his first touchdown "since I was 10 years old playing Pee Wee Football." Inside the Buffalo 10, he slowed down, held the ball out in his massive right paw, and began to strut. Just one more yard now and—*d'oh!*—Buffalo receiver Don Beebe swatted the ball free and through the back of the end zone. Instead of a touchdown, Lett was looking at a touchback. It didn't affect the outcome: Dallas won, 52-17. But it did affect Lett: "How could I hear someone that small and that fast? I was the one making all the noise. Sixty-four yards for *nothin'*!"

February

One for the Ages

February 2, 1995
Duke vs. UNC

Anytime Duke and North Carolina wind up on the same basketball court, you can count on a reaffirmation of why you fell in love with college hoops in the first place. And if there were a Hall of Fame for basketball games, this one would be in it. The Blue Devils were outgunned and without Coach K, who was recovering from back surgery, but they waged a furious battle against the hated Tar Heels nonetheless. Duke overcame a 17-point deficit and built a 12-point lead, which it subsequently lost before pushing the game into overtime. In the first OT, they were down 8 with 28 seconds to go, but rallied and tied the game again on Jeff Capel's frantic 30-footer as time ran out. It was only after Duke's Greg Newton missed a put-back as time expired in the second OT that Carolina was able to look up and see a 102-100 victory.

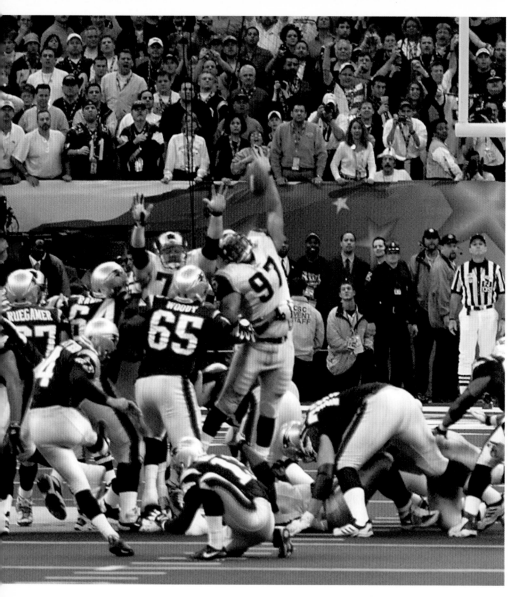

The Leg Man

February 3, 2002
Adam Vinatieri

There were 48 yards between the Patriots and their first Super Bowl victory. Tom Brady had done his job, moving the ball down the field and spiking it with seven ticks left and the score tied 17-17 against the heavily favored Rams. Onto the field trotted Pats kicker Adam Vinatieri, the game hanging on his right leg. The instant the ball left his foot, Vinatieri started jumping. He knew it was dead center and plenty long enough to split the uprights, and he knew his team had won, 20-17, because the scoreboard clock read 0:00.

Counter Punch

February 5, 2006
Willie Parker

The Steelers were nursing a 7-3 lead over the Seahawks as the second half of Super Bowl XL got under way, and if the opening half was any indicator, this one figured to be a snooze fest, too. But just two snaps into it, Pittsburgh running back Willie Parker turned one of the Steelers' bread-and-butter plays—a right counter off guard Alan Faneca—into the longest TD run in Super Bowl history. Sprung by a thunderous clearing block from the 6'5", 307-pound Faneca, Parker found a 75-yard path down the right sideline. "When I saw him running, I knew I couldn't catch that man," Steelers tackle Max Starks said. "I'd see him in the end zone." It was the key play in the Steelers' 21-10 win and their fifth Super Bowl title.

Iron Woman

February 6, 1982
Julie Moss

To call the 140.6-mile swim-bike-and-run Ironman Triathlon in Hawaii grueling is to suggest that Everest is pretty high. In the final, running leg—a full marathon—Julie Moss was eight minutes ahead of Kathleen McCartney with eight miles to go. A quarter-mile from the finish, however, Moss wobbled and then collapsed on the street, and sat staring at it for three full minutes. She willed herself to her feet and crumbled again with 100 yards to go. Then again at 50 yards, and finally, 15 yards from the finish. Moss was still there when McCartney passed her, not even noticing her in a heap on the street. Then, Moss began to crawl and scratch her way toward the finish, eventually completing the ordeal 29 seconds behind McCartney. "Julie Moss gave the world the definition of 'Ironman Spirit,'" said David Yates, president of the World Triathlon Corporation. Better make that Iron*woman* Spirit.

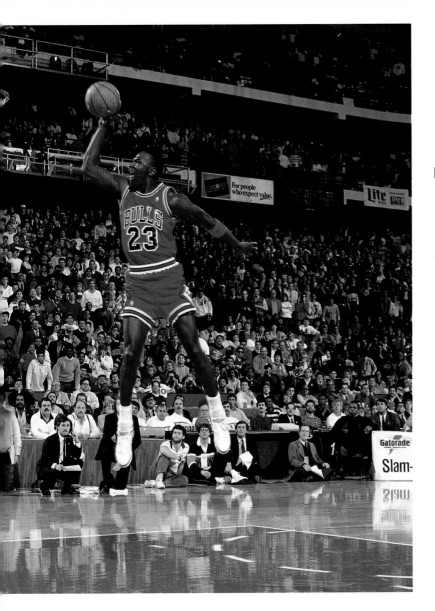

The Skywalker

February 6, 1988
Dominique Wilkins vs. Michael Jordan

In their first NBA All-Star Slam Dunk Contest showdown three years earlier, Dominique Wilkins had schooled rookie Michael Jordan. But this time the event took place in Chicago and the whole house was rooting for the man they now simply called Michael. Wilkins managed a couple of perfect-50 dunks, but a two-handed windmill on his final try netted him only 45. Jordan went to the far end of the floor with a chance to win—as long as he got at least 49 points. "I looked up into the box seats and came across the guy who started it all, Dr. J," Jordan said afterward. "He told me to go back all the way, go the length of the floor, then take off from the free throw line." Erving had pulled off that very move in the 1976 dunk competition. Jordan's version included a double clutch in midair; the slam gave him a perfect 50 to win.

No Fight Left in Him

February 7, 1997
Oliver McCall vs. Lennox Lewis

Two and a half years earlier, when heavyweights Lennox Lewis and Oliver McCall met in a WBC title bout in London, McCall pulled off a stunning two-round upset. This time, things went weird fast. After getting hammered in the first three rounds, McCall refused to fight in the fourth and fifth, aimlessly wandered the ring, and eventually began to sob. The ref, Mills Lane, later said, "I thought he was playing possum. But then I saw his lips start to quiver and I thought, 'My God, is he crying?'" Lewis got the TKO and the WBC heavyweight title.

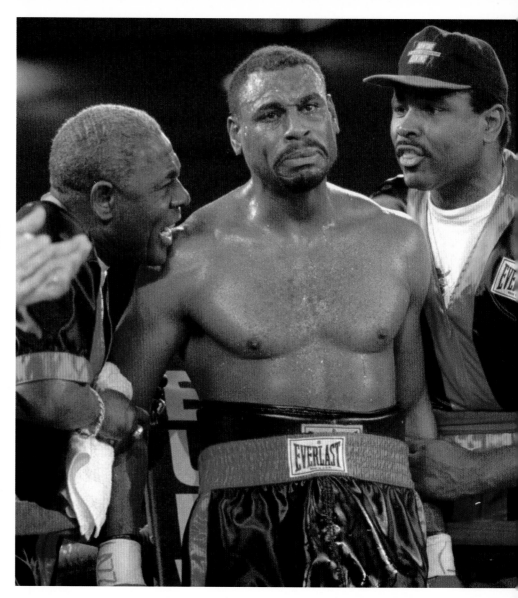

A Little Jam Session

February 8, 1986
Spud Webb

He was 5'7" and even standing still he couldn't palm the ball, but Spud Webb—so nicknamed after his resemblance to Sputnik as a boy, when he had very little hair—sure could throw it down. At the slam dunk contest during NBA All-Star Game weekend, Webb faced off against the defending dunkmeister, Dominique Wilkins. Webb got the crowd behind him with a two-hand reverse dunk made all the more remarkable by the fact that the ball hit him on the head after going through the hoop. He tied Wilkins in the second round, and the pair of Hawks faced off in the finals. Webb performed a 360° corkscrew dunk for a perfect score of 50, then repeated that perfection on his second and final dunk of the contest by bouncing the ball off the floor, spinning around in mid-air, and jamming it home. At 6'8", Wilkins may have started off more than a foot closer to the rim, but Webb ended up with two more points and walked off with the slam dunk title.

Do You Believe in Magic?

February 9, 1992
Magic Johnson

Three months earlier, Magic Johnson, one of basketball's best, most famous, and most beloved players, announced that he was HIV positive and was retiring. But he would have another moment in the NBA sun, the All-Star Game. There was no shortage of controversy—some felt his appearance was dangerous, others felt he didn't belong because he'd retired. He answered them all with 25 points, 9 assists, and 1 lift of the MVP Award, all racked up in 29 minutes of floor time. "People with this virus can live on," Johnson said after the game. "That's the message. They can run; they can jump. Second of all, you don't have to worry about me playing. You can't get it from hugging, kissing, elbows, and high fives. Life doesn't stop because something happens to you."

Twisting Again

February 10, 2002
Kelly Clark

During practice three days before the Olympic women's halfpipe, American Kelly Clark attempted the maneuver known as a McTwist—a 540° inverted rotation—and ended up sprawled on the ground, staring at the sky for 20 minutes as she felt her back begin to swell. But on game day, Clark popped a song by blink-182 into her mp3 player and dropped into the 426-foot pipe for her final run. She went huge, sticking the McTwist and grabbing the gold.

For Whom the Bell Tolls

February 11, 1990
Buster Douglas vs. Mike Tyson

In 37 bouts, Mike Tyson had never lost. All but four of those times, his opponent ended up on the canvas. That's why nobody could have thought for even a second that his reign as heavyweight champion would be ended in Tokyo by Buster Douglas, an utterly unremarkable fighter. Even fewer thought so when Tyson unleashed his full fury on Douglas in the eighth, rocking him to the canvas with a vicious uppercut toward the end of the round. Douglas staggered to his feet at the count of nine just as the bell saved him. But only two rounds later, Douglas went on the offensive. In the 10th, he unloaded a four-punch combo that sent Tyson down and his mouthpiece flying across the ring. As the bell sounded at the count of 10, Tyson found himself in an unfamiliar place: on the floor.

The Fix Was In

February 11, 2002
Jamie Sale and David Pelletier

In the most surreal moment in figure skating since Nancy Kerrigan got whacked (*see* January 6, 1994), a French judge jiggered her scores to ensure that the Russian pair of Anton Sikharulidze and Elena Berezhnaya won the Olympic gold medal over the clear winners, Canada's Jamie Sale and David Pelletier. After a near-perfect performance, the Canadians looked on in disbelief as their not-as-perfect scores were announced. On the telecast, the revered Scott Hamilton gasped, "How did that happen?" His fellow host, Sandra Bezic, declared, "I'm embarrassed for our sport right now." After much brouhaha, finger-pointing, and accusations of vote swapping (and the accompanying denials), the French judge, Marie-Reine Le Gougne, finally fessed up that the head of the French Skating Federation, Didier Gailhaguet, had told her before the event to put the Russians first, allegedly as a *quid pro quo* to ensure French skaters would win the ice dance competition. Six days later, the IOC awarded a second gold medal to the Canadians.

The Flying Tomato's Red Glare

February 12, 2006
Shaun White

One-man extreme sports juggernaut Shaun White had a problem before he dropped into the halfpipe for his first run at the Torino Olympics: He felt "Olympic-y." We think that means he had butterflies. But they were dispatched long before his ultrasmooth gold medal-winning finals run. A frontside air, a McTwist, two 1080s, and another pair of 900s put the Flying Tomato atop the standings and a gold medal around his neck.

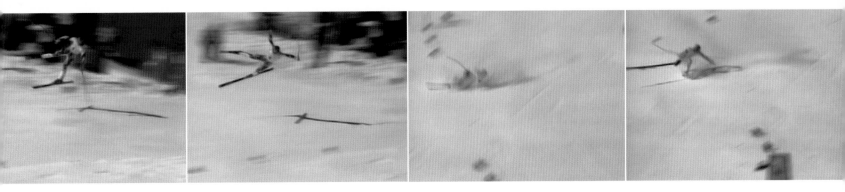

Gate of Hell

February 13, 1998
Hermann Maier

Hermann Maier—Austria's feared Herminator, a name he earned for his dominance of World Cup skiing—was flying along the downhill course at the Nagano Winter Olympics looking for gold. Like many before him, he didn't realize a gate had been moved two meters before the race started but after the skiers had inspected the run. Maier, one of 15 in the field of 43 skiers who didn't finish, wiped out at the gate, but The Herminator earned the most style points. In a crash seen 'round the world, he flipped at least 30 feet in the air and landed on his shoulder before plowing through two ski fences. But his time in Japan wasn't a complete wipeout. A few days later, Maier left for home with two gold medals around his neck, for the super G and the giant slalom.

Falling Hero

February 14, 1988
Dan Jansen

On the morning of the 500-meter Olympic speed skating race, top American skater Dan Jansen, 22, spoke to his sister Jane on the telephone. She died a few hours later, after a 13-month fight with leukemia. Jansen took to the ice anyway, and dedicated the race to her. Perhaps trying too hard, perhaps overcome by grief, Jansen felt his skates fly out from under him on the first turn—and with them, his chance for gold. When he got to his feet, Jansen simply glided along the ice in a world of his own.

Time to Make the Donut

February 15, 1998
Dale Earnhardt

On his 21st attempt, The Intimidator finally won the Daytona 500 and celebrated by inscribing his car's number 3 into the infield with his spinning tires. Admiring his landscaping, Earnhardt said to the press, "I'm pretty good at writin', huh?"

Packing Heat

February 15, 2006
Jason McElwain

With four minutes left in the final home game of the season, Jason McElwain, the devoted manager of the Greece Athena High basketball team in Greece, New York, was finally given the chance to play. After an air ball on his first attempt from the field, the 17-year-old McElwain, who is autistic, caught fire. He nailed six three-pointers and finished with 20 points in those four minutes. The crowd went wild. After being carried off the court on his teammates' shoulders, McElwain said, accurately, "I was hot as a pistol."

Speed Demon

February 16, 1984
Bill Johnson

Bill Johnson could sure talk the talk; coming into the Winter Olympics in Sarajevo, the downhill skier declared, "They should hand the gold medal to me. Everyone else can fight for second." It was vintage Johnson: the speed demon was famously arrogant at the ripe age of 23. This time, Johnson put his skiing where his mouth was and clocked a blistering descent in the men's downhill, averaging 63 mph on the 3,066-meter course, beating his nearest competitor by more than a quarter-second.

All Fall Down

February 16, 2002
Apolo Ohno

Top American speed skater Apolo Anton Ohno, gunning for gold in the Winter Olympics at Salt Lake City, grabbed the lead with two laps to go in the 1,000-meter final and held it to within seconds of the finish. With just 20 meters to go, however, Li Jiajun of China tried a roller-derby move to pass Ohno on the outside and made contact. Then South Korean Ahn Hyun-Soo made a move and touched Li; his stumble started the dominos falling. Down went Li, down went Ahn, and down went Ohno. Steven Bradbury of Australia, who was in last place, zipped past the pile of skaters on the way to gold. Ohno picked himself up and scrambled across the finish line for the silver.

Overcooked Hot Dog

February 17, 2006
Lindsey Jacobellis

Twenty-year-old Lindsey Jacobellis was on the second-to-last jump in the first Olympic women's snowboard cross finals and was clear of her nearest competitor by about 50 yards. Looking to cap off her big moment in high style, Jacobellis grabbed her board in midair and angled it to the right. Then all frozen hell broke loose—she later said a wind kicked up. Whatever, Jacobellis lost her balance and fell on her butt, from where she watched Tanja Frieden of Switzerland fly past for the gold. Jacobellis hopped back up to score the silver and retained a positive attitude, saying, "I was having fun. I wanted to share my enthusiasm with the crowd."

Golden Moment

February 18, 1994
Dan Jansen

It was beginning to look like World Cup champion speed skater Dan Jansen would never get an Olympic medal. He fell twice in 1988, and only got to 4th place in the 1992 500-meter race. Earlier in these 1994 games in Lillehammer, Norway, Jansen again slipped and touched the ice, plummeting to eighth place in the 500-meter competition. His last chance was the 1,000 meters, where he was not favored. Instead, he smoked the field with a world-record time of 1:12:43—plenty good for gold. Jansen took a victory lap holding his baby daughter, who bore the name of his departed sister, Jane (*see* February 14, 1988). There wasn't a dry eye in the house.

Death of The Intimidator

February 18, 2001
Dale Earnhardt

He was known as The Intimidator because he drove hard and drove to win. The fans loved him because he was the last of the old-school guys who ate spark plugs for breakfast and washed them down with motor oil. At the Daytona 500, Dale Earnhardt didn't have a chance to win, but that didn't stop him from trying for the best possible finish with a pass in the final turn of the final lap. As Dale Jr. and Michael Waltrip sped bumper to bumper toward the checkered flag, Sr. tried to push past Sterling Marlin and take third place. A split-second later, either slight contact with Marlin's car or a sudden shift in aerodynamics caused Ironhead—as Earnhardt Sr. was also known—to smash into the wall. The track doctor arrived at the scene just moments later, but quickly saw that Earnhardt was dying. CPR was attempted with Earnhardt still in the car, and on the way to the hospital. The man everyone, including himself, believed was too tough to be killed in a crash was pronounced dead at 5:16 p.m.

Do You Believe in Miracles?

February 22, 1980
USA vs. USSR

Americans hadn't been so button-busting proud about a victory since they were the first to get to the moon. When the clock ran out on the U.S. Olympic hockey team's 4-3 semifinals win over the fearsome Soviet Union, the shaggy-haired college kids who made up the squad flooded the ice and instantly and inextricably became linked to the word "miracle." It was a perfect moment, a marriage of hope and improbability that became extinct when professionals were later allowed in Olympic competition.

Chair Man of the Boards

February 23, 1985
Bobby Knight

Just a few minutes into a game against Purdue, Indiana coach Bobby Knight shouted an obscenity at a referee (gasp!), who promptly slapped him with a T. Mt. Knight erupted, grabbing a chair and flinging it onto the court, where it skidded in front of Purdue's Steve Reid at the foul line. That was another T, which was followed by another before Knight left the floor for the night. It wasn't Knight's first on-court outburst, of course, and it wouldn't be his last. Did it fire up his Hoosiers? Not this night: Purdue 72, Indiana 63.

Great Expectations

February 24, 1982
Wayne Gretzky

He was just 21, but in the 64th game of the season, Wayne Gretzky scored his 77th goal of the season, breaking Phil Esposito's 11-year-old record. The goal, which came in the third period, was unassisted, and Gretzky scored on his next two shots as well, ending the game with a hat trick. After the game, Espo, who grew up in Sault Ste. Marie, Ontario, recounted the story of the day his father told him he'd seen a teenager named Gretzky playing for the Sault Ste. Marie Greyhounds "who will break all your records someday." Mr. Esposito evidently knew a thing or two about hockey.

Shameless ESPN Classic Plug No. 1

February 25, 1964
Cassius Clay vs. Sonny Liston

Sure, a lot has happened since ESPN was launched in September 1979—you're holding proof of that. But we couldn't resist taking a deep bow to some of the greatest moments of all time, starting with this one from The Greatest of All Time. In the first Clay-Liston bout, the 22-year-old, poetry-mouthed Cassius Clay ran rings around 31-year-old Sonny Liston, throwing swift combinations, opening a cut under Liston's left eye in the third, and dancing away from the top-heavy champ's searching fists. When the bell sounded signalling the seventh round, Liston sat in his corner, head bowed. That's when Clay, the new heavyweight champion, shouted at reporters, "I shook up the world! I shook up the world!"

Stockton Delivers

February 26, 1996
John Stockton to Karl Malone

Unitas to Berry. Montana to Rice. Magic to Kareem. Butch to Sundance. And now, add another pairing to the Alchemy/Synergy Hall of Fame: Stockton to Malone. With a routine pass for a routine 16-footer by Karl Malone, John Stockton became the first NBA player to notch 11,000 assists, most of them to Malone. By the time he retired in 2003, Stockton's name stood firmly atop the assists category with 15,806—more than 5,000 beyond Mark Jackson's second-place total.

Cub at Play

February 27, 1992
Tiger Woods

At 16, Tiger Woods was the youngest player ever to tee it up with the big boys in a pro tournament. The logical place for a star to be born was the Los Angeles Open, of course, and it didn't hurt that Woods, the U.S. Junior Amateur champ, lived nearby in Cypress. Given a sponsor's exemption into the field, Woods shot a one-over 72 in the first round at Riviera. The future champion missed the cut, but not before he got to practice some postgame chatter, saying, "I hit it terrible but somehow scraped it around."

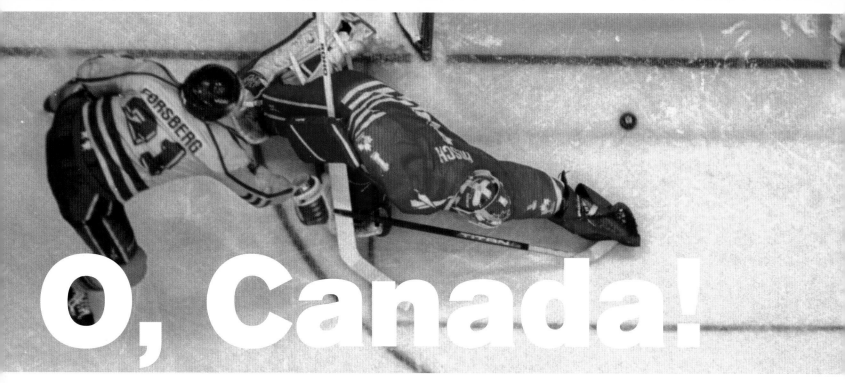

O, Canada!

February 27, 1994
Sweden vs. Canada

It had been 42 years since the country synonymous with hockey excellence won Olympic gold. Now, facing off against Sweden in the finals at Lillehammer, Canada's last, best hope was a single shot. After a 2-2 tie in regulation, one scoreless overtime, and one shoot out round that produced two goals for each side, the game was to be decided by a sudden-death shoot out. Sweden's Peter Forsberg decided to try a shot he'd seen on TV five years earlier. A lefty, he angled to his forehand side, pulling the goalie with him, and just as he was on top of the net, Forsberg dipped hard to his backhand side and tapped in the goal with ease. Forsberg said later that he'd tried that move maybe three times—and never made it. For Canada, Paul Kariya now went with the strategy that netted the first two shoot out goals for his team—high to the glove side of Sweden's Tommy Salo. But the shot wasn't high enough and it bounced off the Swede's pads. Oh, my, Canada …

March

A Rule's a Rule

March 1, 1991
Paul Azinger

After posting a 65 in the second round of the Doral-Ryder Open, Paul Azinger said, "I was playing good enough to win." Key word: "was." On the final hole of his first-round 69, Azinger had to play a shot from a water hazard. While assuming his stance, Azinger moved a few pebbles as he dug in with his feet. An alert television viewer in Colorado phoned tour officials and informed them that the very integrity of the game was being mashed beneath Zinger's spikes, citing Rule 13-4, subsection C, of the Rules of Golf, which states that before making a stroke at a ball that is in a hazard, a player must not "touch or move a loose impediment lying in or touching the hazard." Those pebbles under Azinger's feet as he took his stance? They moved. Because he did not declare a penalty for his violation of 13-4c, the 69 Azinger signed for on Thursday wasn't really a 69—and that, in turn, meant automatic disqualification. "It was a subconscious thing, to dig my foot in there to get a stance," said Azinger after he got the DQ. "It had zero influence on the shot that I played." Tell it to the R&A and the USGA, Paul.

Century Mark

March 2, 1962
Wilt Chamberlain

Shameless ESPN Classic Plug No. 2: No playoff implications, no television, no New York sportswriters. Just a 7'1" pivot man turning in the only individual triple-digit scoring effort in NBA history. In a Warriors-Knicks game played in Hershey, Pa., Chamberlain broke his own mark of 78 points in the fourth quarter; when he scored his never-before-even-imagined 100th point with 46 seconds left, the Chocolate Town crowd, frenzied after imbibing so much offense, stormed the court. After the Warriors finished off the Knicks, 169-147, Chamberlain said, "It was my greatest game." It was *anyone's* greatest game.

Sis-Boom-Ouch!

March 5, 2006
Kristi Yamaoka

A little tumble from the top of the pyramid couldn't dampen Southern Illinois cheerleader Kristi Yamaoka's school spirit. The 15-foot fall gave her a cracked neck vertebra and a concussion, but even as she was wheeled off the court on a stretcher, she continued to cheer to the Salukis' fight song. Despite an emphasis on safety in practice, Yamaoka's teammates were philosophical about their occupation's hazards. "Things happen," one of them said later. "Girls get dropped."

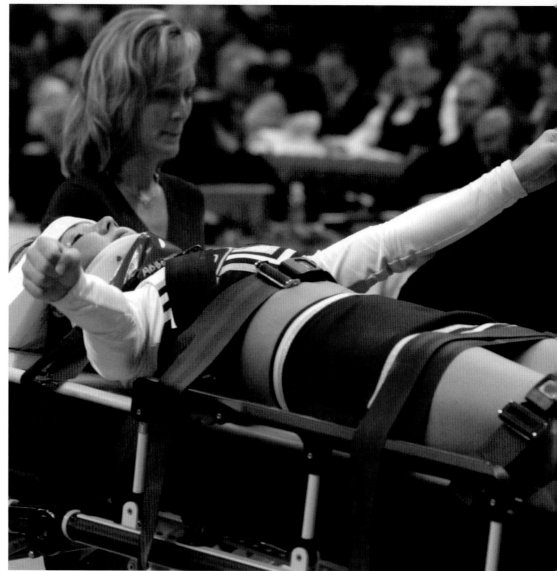

A Pyrrhic Victory

March 10, 2006
Cuba vs. Puerto Rico

The night before Cuba took the field against Puerto Rico in Round 1 of the World Baseball Classic, a high-ranking member of the Cuban delegation had been booted from the stadium during the Cuba-Netherlands game for confronting a fan carrying an anti-Castro sign. The Cubans threatened to pull out of the WBC in protest. Good thing they didn't. Puerto Rico, with a roster sporting about $80 million of major-league talent, shellacked their Caribbean neighbors 12-2 in a no-contest highlighted by homers from Carlos Beltran, Alex Cintrón, and Bernie Williams. But five days later, in Round 2, Cuba got sweet revenge with a 4-3 win over Puerto Rico that sent the Cubanos into the semifinals, where they beat the Dominican Republic to advance to the finals. They eventually lost to Japan in the finals and finished second in the 2006 WBC, but they were undisputed Kings of the Caribbean. So much for that $80M talent edge.

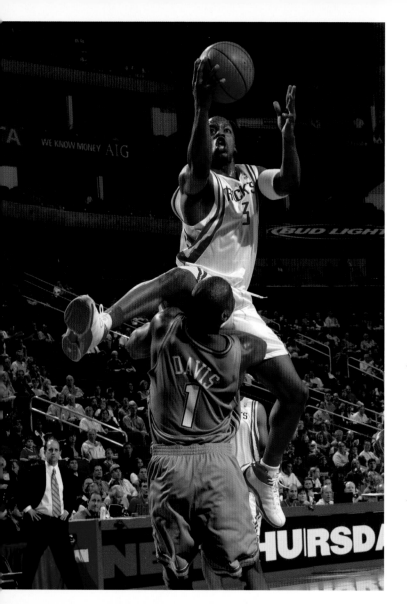

I Said Move!

March 11, 2004
Steve Francis

Two of Steve Francis' 19 points for Houston in a 97-86 win over the Hornets came when Baron Davis just wouldn't get out of his way. Francis wasn't bothered: he went right over—*way* over—Davis and slammed home a killer dunk that left the Baron reeling.

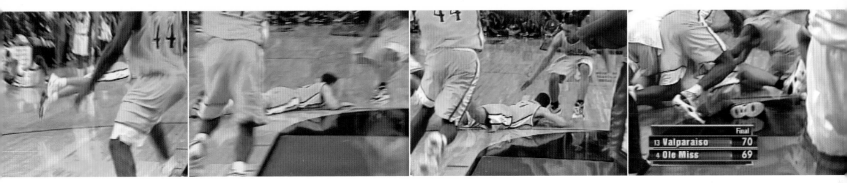

The Longest Play

March 13, 1998
Bryce Drew

Thirteenth-seeded Valparaiso was down 69-67, and with just 2.5 seconds and the length of the court left in the game, in perfect position to do what everyone thought they would do: lose to fourth-seeded Ole Miss in the first round of the NCAAs. But Valpo had a secret weapon: a three-point play they called Pacer, which they'd practiced every day, all season long. Bryce Drew, the shooter on the play, nailed the three about half the time. This turned out to be one of those times. Teammate Jamie Sykes juked the Ole Miss player guarding him on the inbounds pass and lasered the ball three-quarters the length of the court to Bill Jenkins, who made a touch pass to Drew, who then let fly as the clock ran out to give Valpo the 70-69 win. Drew leaped for joy—a horizontal leap that became a victory slide on the hardwood, where he was soon joined by his fellow Crusaders.

Shoot and Run

March 14, 1981
U.S. Reed

The Louisville Cardinals headed into the NCAAs looking to defend their national title. They headed out in the second round, after Arkansas' U.S. Reed made a 49-footer at the buzzer to push the Hogs to a 74-73 win. As soon as the shot fell, Reed walked directly off the court into the locker room, not even joining the pileup of teammates at center court. "When I did the same thing against Texas," explained a smiling Reed, "everybody piled on me and I got hurt a little bit. I didn't want that to happen again."

Slow Mo O

March 14, 1996
Princeton vs. UCLA

In the first round of the NCAA Tournament, defending champion UCLA drew the unenviable task of playing
13th-seeded Princeton. Why unenviable? Because Pete Carril's Tigers were master ballhandlers who ran the most
disciplined, most deliberate—okay, *slowest*—offense in the country. How slow? Slow enough to drive opponents stark
raving mad. With 3.9 seconds left to play, the score tied 41-41, and UCLA knowing what was coming, the Tigers ran
one of Carril's patented backdoor plays and freshman Gabe Lewullis laid in a bounce pass from Steve Goodrich to
send the Bruins back to Westwood—the first defending champs to bow out in the first round since Indiana in 1988.

Velvet Gloves

March 16, 1996
Christy Martin vs. Deirdre Gogarty

There was just one thing that saved the 1.1 million suckers who paid-per-view to see Mike Tyson beat a trembling Frank Bruno into submission in a stinker of a fight: Christy Martin. Martin hammered Deirdre Gogarty in a bloody bit of business that made up for the Tyson-Bruno yawn at the top of the card. Gogarty broke Martin's nose early in the fight, but Martin scored the only knockdown in the second and won the six-round fight by decision. Afterward, her husband/trainer said, "The key to our success is that she's 100% female—she wears high heels, fingernail polish, everything." And packs a powerful right.

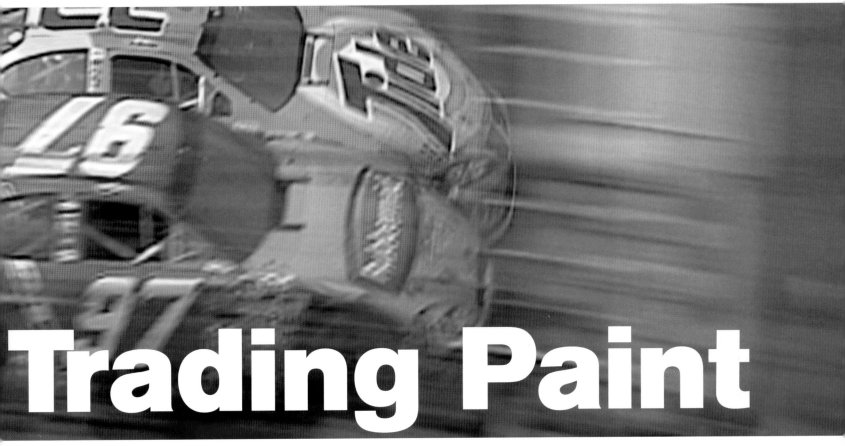

Trading Paint

March 16, 2003
Kurt Busch vs. Ricky Craven

After two laps of neck-and-neck racing between Ricky Craven and Kurt Busch at the end of the Carolina Dodge Dealers 400, it came down to the final turn at Darlington. Exiting the corner, Craven slid down below Busch and the pair roared down the last straightaway, bumping each other—hard—all the way to the checkered flag. Craven took the win by inches—a $^2/_{1,000}$-second margin of victory, the closest since NASCAR started using electronic timing a decade earlier.

Calvary to the Rescue!

March 18, 1999
Casey Calvary

Today, every March Madness fan uses Gonzaga as a synonym for a Cinderella team. But back in 1999, the Bulldogs hadn't yet made a funny-sounding name for themselves. All that changed, however, in the final minute of Gonzaga's Sweet 16 matchup with the sixth-seeded Florida Gators. With 45.7 seconds left, Florida's Greg Stolt buried a three and put the Gators up 72-69. The 10th-seeded Bulldogs didn't panic; when a play they drew up on the sideline didn't materialize, they called a TO with 27.9 seconds left, then made a layup. Florida center Brent Wright traveled after he caught the inbounds pass, and the Bulldogs got the ball back. Quentin Hall put up a running 10-footer and missed, but Casey Calvary tipped in a put-back and Gonzaga won, 73-72. Cinderella was still dancing.

A Whole New Ballgame

March 19, 1995
Michael Jordan

Think of it as a reminder—as if we needed one—of Michael Jordan's greatness. After 17 months of amusing himself on the golf course and playing minor league baseball, he returned to the hardwood to play a game that people paid upward of $700 a ticket to see. That translated to about $100 for each shot Jordan made from the field—against 21 misses—in a 103-96 overtime loss to the Pacers. Jordan, wearing No. 45 (from his junior high days) instead of his familiar 23, played most of the game but was bent over and breathing hard during stoppages, a result of only a handful of Bulls practices and a sign that the only hoops he played during his baseball career was pickup games with teammates. "A lot of guys playing baseball thought they were basketball players," he said. "Maybe kinda like I thought I was a baseball player."

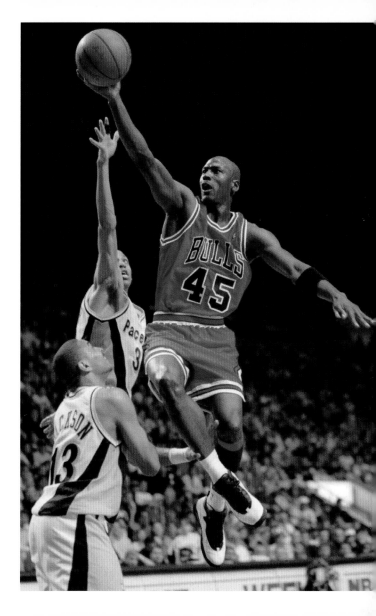

Double Dip

March 19, 2006
Candace Parker

That Tennessee's Lady Vols won their first-round NCAA
Tournament game against Army 102-54 was no surprise.
But hold on a second … and then another one! At 6:12
into the first half, Vols redshirt freshman Candace Parker
threw down this one-hander on a breakaway that was
the first dunk in a women's NCAA Tournament game.
But why settle for one when two are twice as nice? Later
in the game, the 6'4" Parker jammed home another one
from the baseline. Her line for the game: 26 points, 5
rebounds, 7 assists, 4 blocks, 2 steals—and 2 dunks!

Long Shot

March 20, 1981
Wichita State vs. Kansas

The Wichita State Shockers lived up to their nickname in a Sweet 16 game against Kansas in the first meeting of the two schools in 25 years. During that quarter-century, of course, Kansas had the rep as the big basketball school. But in this contest, Wichita State forwards Antoine Carr and Cliff Levingston called the shots. As the game wound down and the Kansas defense packed in to defend against Carr and Levingston, Shockers sixth man Mike Jones came off the bench. With 47 seconds to go and his team down by three, Jones banged home a 25-footer. With four seconds left and his team down by one, Jones dropped another bomb to win the game, 66-65. "I looked at the clock and saw I had to let it go," Jones said. "We needed it. Somebody had to make it." Especially since you get only one chance every 25 years.

Sweet to Sour

March 20, 1994
Boston College vs. UNC

With 13 straight Sweet 16 appearances, Dean Smith's UNC squad had Tar Heels fans frothing at the mouth for a national championship, especially with the arrival of superfreshmen Rasheed Wallace and Jerry Stackhouse. But a stunning 75-72 defeat at the hands of Boston College in the East Regional sent that Sweet 16 streak home crying. It was a landmark game for the Heels, one that signaled the danger of expecting too much too soon of talented freshmen, instead of breaking them into the program the way Smith usually did.

Upsetters Upset

March 21, 2003
Drew Nicholas

After sinking two free throws with five seconds left, UNC-Wilmington looked like it was going to pull off a first-round NCAA upset for the second straight year, this time by one point over defending champs Maryland. But after inbounding the ball at their own end, the Terps quickly worked it up the court and into the hands of Drew Nicholas, who let fly a running, fallaway three-pointer from right in front of his own bench. "My instincts took over," Nicholas said afterward. "The rest is history." History tells us that Maryland won, 75-73.

Just a Sec

March 22, 1990
UConn vs. Clemson

With one tick left on the clock in the NCAA East Regional semifinals and his UConn Huskies trailing by one, Tate George hauled down a court-length pass, squared up to shoot a fundamentally sound J, and nailed it. Final score: UConn 71, Clemson 70. *Mush!*

Wildcats Rein Bulldogs

March 22, 2003
Arizona vs. Gonzaga

A team less comfortable in glass slippers than the Gonzaga Bulldogs might have been intimidated by a top-seeded Wildcats outfit packed with stars like Channing Frye, Luke Walton, Salim Stoudamire, and Jason Gardner, here putting a shot over Winston Brooks. But the Bulldogs ferociously pushed the second-round Tournament game into two overtimes, and were set for another Cinderella star-turn until Blake Stepp missed an eight-foot put-back, and Arizona held on to win, 96-95. The players knew the game was not to be forgotten no matter that David this time failed to beat Goliath. "That," Gardner said after the game, "was definitely an ESPN Classic."

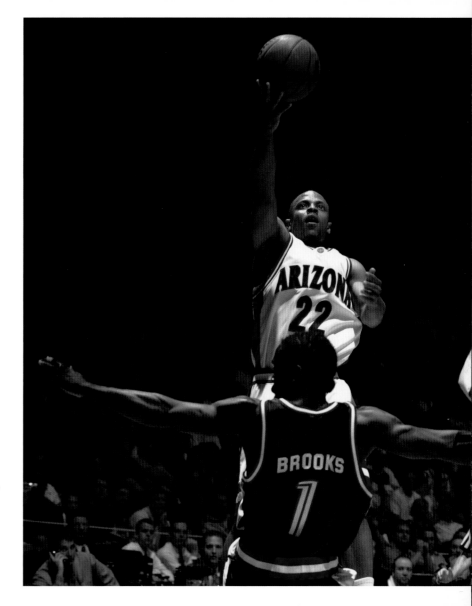

Even Devils Get the Blues

March 23, 2006
LSU vs. Duke

Something funny happened to top-seeded Duke and wonderboy J.J. Redick on their way to the NCAA championship: they ran into a bunch of hungry LSU Tigers in the regional semifinals. All game long, LSU freshman guard Garrett Temple stuck to Redick like a refrigerator magnet, forcing the Blue Devils' hottest hand into 3-for-18 shooting in a 62-54 upset. "He's long," said Redick of the 6'5" Temple. "It was just a very physical game. He did a good job of contesting my jump shots, and when I did drive, they had shot-blockers back there." Redick didn't get much help: overall, Duke shot 18 of 65 from the field to miss the Elite 8 for a second consecutive year.

He Scoops!
He Scores!

March 24, 1996
Mike Legg

In a quarterfinal game of the NCAA hockey championships against Minnesota, Michigan's Mike Legg picked up the puck with his stick as if he were playing lacrosse, then moved from behind the net and flung it into the net like, well, a lacrosse shot on ice. No wonder it won an ESPY.

No-Fly Zone

March 24, 2001
Randy Johnson

A dove who wasn't wearing a batting helmet crossed paths with a 97 mph Randy Johnson fastball during a D-Backs spring training game against the Giants. The bird exploded like an egg in a microwave oven. The batter, Calvin Murray, had no sympathy for the late fowl and lobbied the ump to call the pitch a ball. Said Arizona manager Bob Brenly after the game, "Randy is going to get arrested for hunting dove out of season or something."

Triple the Fun

March 25, 2006
Kimmie Meissner

Swirling around the ice to the tune of "Belkis, Queen of Sheba," 16-year-old Kimmie Meissner landed seven triple jumps in her long program—more than anyone else in the competition—to score an upset win in the World Figure Skating Championships. "It blew the rest of my programs out of the water," Meissner said. "That was definitely the best that I could have done." It was her first time competing in the Worlds and her first year skating in the sport's upper echelon. "When I hit my first jump," said Meissner, "I was like, I can do it." And so she did.

Now's the Time to Fight

March 26, 2005
Arizona vs. Illinois

With 4:04 left in an Elite 8 game against Arizona, the Fighting Illini found themselves in an unfamiliar situation. Illinois, which had lost only once all season, trailed by 15, and the Final Four suddenly seemed very far away. Then they began to fight, cutting Arizona's lead to 8 with 1:03 on the clock. The next 25 seconds were straight out of a made-for-TV movie: Luther Head popped a three; Dee Brown, following a mid-court steal, laid one in; and Deron Williams hit another one from behind the arc, knotting the game at 80 all. Illinois held on for a 90-89 overtime win.

Cinderella Stumbles

March 26, 2005
Louisville vs. West Virginia

Seventh-seeded West Virginia was the lovable underdog in this NCAA Tournament, and when they played Louisville for free tickets to the Final Four, the Mountaineers seemed ready to return all that love. They rained threes on Louisville in the first half, at one point holding a 20-point lead. They still led by half that margin with 5:27 left in the game. Things looked grim for the Cards: their best player, Francisco Garcia, fouled out with 4:02 to go, and Taquan Dean, another top gun, was suffering from severe cramps. But Rick Pitino's squad hung tough, and with 38 seconds left, Louisville native Larry O'Bannon drove to the hoop for two that tied the game at 77-77 and forced OT. Just 23 seconds into the extra period, O'Bannon drained two free throws that gave Louisville its first lead since 3-0, and the Cards never trailed again. Final score: Louisville 93, West Virginia 85.

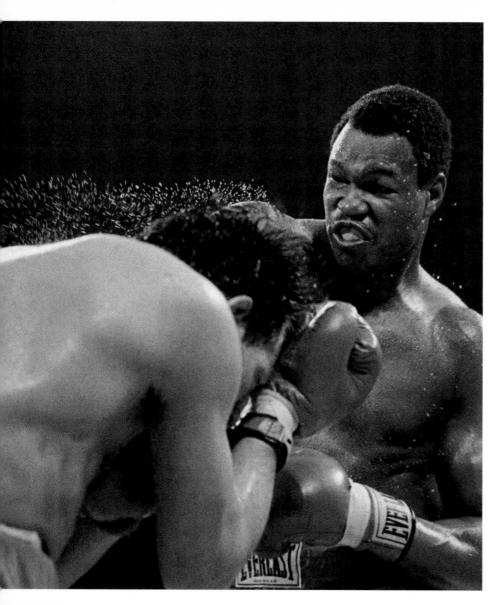

Home Schooled

March 27, 1983
Larry Holmes vs. Lucien Rodriguez

They called Larry Holmes the Easton Assassin, because he lived in that little hardscrabble eastern Pennsylvania city when he grew up. But Holmes learned the sweet science in nearby Scranton, where he fought his first professional fight and eight others, and so he found it fitting to defend his heavyweight championship in front of the Scranton fans. It wasn't Vegas, for sure, but Holmes won a unanimous 12-round decision over Lucien Rodriguez. "I would've rather had this title fight at the C.Y.C.," Holmes said of the Catholic Youth Center where he had his first bout, "but it only holds about 4,000 people."

Onward Christian's Soldiers

March 28, 1992
Christian Laettner

Coach K's Blue Devils were hanging by a thread against Kentucky in overtime in the East Regional finals. With 2.1 seconds left in the game and the Wildcats up 103-102, Christian Laettner, in heavy traffic, managed to snag Grant Hill's lofted inbounds pass and, in one swell swoop, spin and shoot from the top of the foul line. As the jumper fell for a one-point victory, Laettner, who'd executed the shot with the icy nerve of a hit man, leapt once again, this time into the arms of his teammates. Duke was headed to the Final Four for the fifth straight season. And Laettner was headed to the Highlight Reel Hall of Fame.

Jordan: Act I, Scene 1

March 29, 1982
Michael Jordan

With 61,612 sets of eyes looking on from the seats of the Louisiana Superdome, North Carolina freshman Michael Jordan hit a 16-footer with 15 seconds left to play, pushing the Tar Heels past Georgetown 63-62 and giving Dean Smith his first NCAA championship. It also gave Jordan his first great moment on the national stage. "That's *the* shot," Jordan remembered 20 years later. "That's the one that initiated everything."

Triple-Double Eagle

March 29, 2003
Dwyane Wade

At halftime of the Midwest Regional final against Kentucky, Marquette's Dwyane Wade told his teammates, "Leave your hearts on the court." No one heeded that advice more than Wade himself, who earned his first triple-double as he turned in one of the NCAA Tournament's most memorable performances. Wade's totals included 29 points, 11 rebounds, and 11 assists, but the numbers barely tell how his game affected the rest of the Golden Eagles. The 83-69 rout of the No. 1 seed Wildcats lifted them into the Final Four, where Kansas would soon teach Marquette what being routed feels like.

Air Ball

March 30, 1981
Isiah Thomas

With an impish grin that belied a killer heart, Indiana's Isiah Thomas gave his school its fourth NCAA title with a second half against North Carolina that defied reason. Thomas scored 19 of his 23 points after the break, and more important, made four steals. The first two of those steals came in the first 90 seconds after halftime and dramatically shifted the momentum of a close game. As time expired, with Indiana on top, 63-50, Thomas had the ball in his hands and he threw it straight up, as high as he could. Sometimes, there's nothing finer than a good air ball.

Smart Move

March 30, 1987
Keith Smart

Bobby Knight was 2-0 in NCAA championship games, but that spotless record was in peril as his Hoosiers squared off against Syracuse. Indiana trailed 73-72 with five seconds left when Keith Smart spotted up for a wide-open 17-footer and knocked it down. For reasons that can never be explained, the Orange let the clock round down to :01 before calling a timeout. Too late. Smart picked off Derrick Coleman's inbounds pass and the game was over. "It'll sink in next week," Smart said afterward. "I couldn't really go berserk at the time because there was still time on the clock and a lot of games have been lost with one second on the clock." Just ask Syracuse.

Perfectly Seasoned

March 31, 2002
UConn Women

The 29,619 warm bodies piled into the Alamodome for the women's NCAA final had come to see perfection—and they got what they came for. The UConn Huskies beat the Oklahoma Sooners 82-70 to win the national title and cap a dream 39-0 season. Only Tennessee's 1998 champs (39-0) could claim the same number of victories in a season. UConn's Swin Cash led the way with 20 points and 13 rebounds and was named the Final Four's Most Outstanding Player.

April

Patience Pays Off

April 1, 1985
Villanova vs. Georgetown

That Villanova was even in the NCAA final against Georgetown, the nation's top team, was something of an upset. Sure, Nova had some talent, plus a famously cagey coach in Rollie Massimino, but they'd lost 10 regular-season games and were unranked heading into March Madness. And now, in the championship game, they faced the best and most swarming defense in the land: a Georgetown that scowled, scared, and hurried its opponents into 39% shooting while recording 35 wins. But in the second half, Villanova outwitted and outwaited the Hoyas, settling only for perfect shots—a luxury they could afford in what was the last NCAA Tournament game played without a shot clock. Villanova shot 22-of-28 from the field, and in the second half they missed only once in 10 shots. Easy Ed Pinckney, the 6'9" Villanova center, outscored and outrebounded the mammoth Patrick Ewing, and it was Pinckney's cat-quick moves to the hoop early in the second half that kept his team in the game. Villanova won, 66-64, in what is still considered the greatest upset in Tournament history. "Georgetown was supposed to win easy," said Nova point guard Gary McLain. "Some of the papers said maybe we should go out to dinner and just let Georgetown celebrate. But once the game starts, all those things don't mean anything."

Slam at the Dance

April 1, 1991
Grant Hill

Many observers questioned whether Duke could recover from an emotional win over UNLV in the Final Four to knock off Kansas in the final. Less than three minutes into the game, the Dukies answered those questions when Bobby Hurley floated what looked to be a too-high alley-oop toward freshman Grant Hill. All Hill did was launch his 6'8" frame into the sky, use his full wingspan to snatch the ball with his right hand, and thunder it home. The dunk gave the Blue Devils an early 7-1 lead, but more important, it let Kansas know it was in for a long night. At the end of it, Coach K took home his first national championship, 72-65.

Jimmy V-ictory

April 4, 1983
NC State vs. Houston

About as much of a chance as a Popsicle in a sauna—that's what everybody said North Carolina State had against Houston's Phi Slamma Jamma juggernaut. Everybody was wrong. The Wolfpack clawed back from six down with three minutes left to tie the score. Then, with two seconds on the clock, Dereck Whittenburg desperately heaved up a 35-footer, a total air ball—that somehow landed in the hands of teammate Lorenzo Charles, who jammed it home for a 54-52 win. "It was supposed to be a pass," Whittenburg said with a straight face after the game. No one was in a bigger state of shock than NC State coach Jim Valvano, who sprinted onto the court waving his arms like a madman as the horn sounded. "They're probably tired of hearing me talk about dreaming," a calmer Valvano said of his players after the game. No, Coach. Nobody ever got tired of that.

Manning Among Boys

April 4, 1988
Danny Manning

An effortlessly graceful athlete with strength, speed, and an amazing touch, Danny Manning played the game as if he were born to it. So the 6'10" Kansas forward's 31-point, 18-rebound performance against Oklahoma in the national championship didn't exactly come as a surprise. With the clock running down and the Jayhawks up 73-71, Manning pulled off what was, for him, a routine sequence: he blocked a jumper by OU's Stacey King, then ran the floor to get in position for a layup. Then, with 16 seconds left and Kansas up 78-77, the Jayhawks' Scooter Barry hit one free throw but missed the next. The board was gobbled up by Manning, who was fouled, then went to the line and made both. A couple of plays later, Manning hit two more from the line for good measure. Final score: Manning ... uh, Kansas 83, Oklahoma 79.

Record Wilts Before Him

April 5, 1984
Kareem Abdul-Jabbar

For the better part of 15 seasons, Kareem Abdul-Jabbar played the role of superhero Captain Skyhook, a character named after a shot he invented to devastating effect. Against the Jazz, with 8:53 left in an early spring game, the Captain called for the ball 12 feet from the basket, got it, and let go with his patented human crane shot, clearing the outstretched fingertips of 7'3" Jazz center Mark Eaton. When the ball clipped through the net, it brought the big man's career points total to 31,421, breaking the unbreakable record of Wilt Chamberlain. And Captain Skyhook wasn't done.

Not So Fab Five

April 5, 1993
Chris Webber

The stuff of NCAA legend, Michigan's Fab Five, in their second straight national championship game, treated the basketball-watching world to the most bizarre finish the tournament had ever seen. With 20 seconds left and his team trailing North Carolina 73-71, Chris Webber grabbed a huge defensive rebound, escaped an obvious traveling call, and moved the ball to near his bench, where he quickly called timeout with 11 seconds left. One problem: Michigan had no TOs remaining. The ensuing technical put the Heels on the line for two points that clinched the game and cost Michigan the title game for the second straight year.

Good Night, Gordie

April 6, 1980
Gordie Howe

Gordie Howe decided it was finally time to hang up the skates after playing professional hockey for 32 seasons. Howe, who began his NHL career in 1946 with the Detroit Red Wings, finished it with the freshly minted Hartford Whalers—and finished it in style. At age 52, Howe played all 80 games, and landed his 801st goal in his final regular-season outing.

Passing the Babe

April 8, 1974
Hank Aaron

Shameless ESPN Classic Plug No. 3: The countdown to Babe Ruth's magic No. 714 had taken a break for the winter—Hank Aaron had gotten all the way to 713 before the 1973 season ended—but got right up to speed in 1974. Hammerin' Hank tied The Babe's mark on his first swing of the season in Cincinnati, and then broke it during the Braves' first homestand. Al Downing served a fat pitch up in the fourth inning, Aaron swung, and for the next 11 minutes most of Atlanta took a break to celebrate the shattering of an unbreakable record. Which he'd continue to shatter all the way to No. 755.

Home Not So Sweet

April 8, 1996
Hornets vs. Bulls

The Hornets, fighting for a playoff spot, avenged a humiliating 34-point loss to the Bulls suffered four days earlier. Not only did they beat Chicago 98-97, Charlotte also ended the Bulls' NBA-record 44-game home winning streak. The Bulls hadn't lost at home since March 24, 1995—Michael Jordan's first game at United Center after abandoning baseball and coming out of retirement.

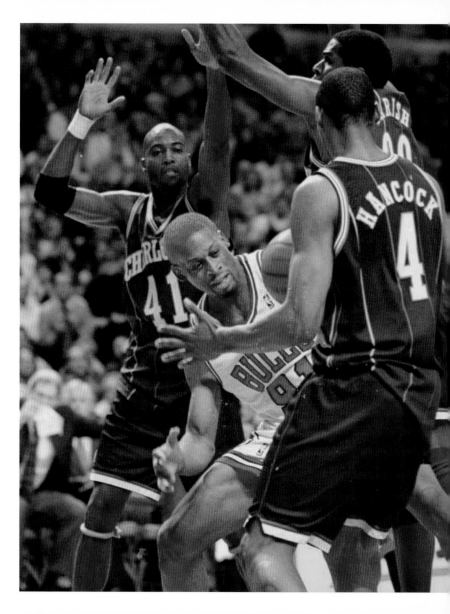

Rhymes with Choke

April 9, 1989
Scott Hoch

On the first sudden-death playoff hole against Nick Faldo for the Masters title, Scott Hoch had a two-foot putt to win it all. He froze over it, seemingly stuck, unable to pull the trigger. In the clubhouse watching on television, Ben Crenshaw, a former Masters champion himself, couldn't stand to watch. "Jesus, hit it!" said Crenshaw to no one in particular. Hoch did, and the near-gimme slid by the hole. "Between my brain and my hand," Hoch said later, "the message got crisscrossed." Faldo, who'd birdied four of the final six holes of regular play in a steady rain, birdied the next playoff hole in the gathering darkness to win the first of his three Masters titles.

Rocky Mountain Highlight

April 10, 2004
University of Denver

From 1958 to 1969, the University of Denver won five national hockey championships—and then the ice cooled off. A quarter-century later, though, the Pioneers were back in the NCAA finals. But their opponent, Maine's Black Bears, did not go quietly. In the final minute of play, Denver held onto a 1-0 lead even though Maine had a two-man advantage. During the furious finish, one Maine shot hit the post, but the rest were turned away by Adam Berkhoel, who had 24 saves on the day. "It's the second-most exciting thing that happened to me today," said Denver defenseman Ryan Caldwell of the win. And the highlight? "I got to meet Bobby Orr in the morning."

Lip Service

April 10, 2005
Tiger Woods

He'd gone 10 majors without winning one of golf's big four events, so when Tiger Woods found himself with a one-shot lead on the 16th hole of the final round of the Masters he—yes, even Tiger—could be forgiven for jerking an iron long and left at the par 3. He couldn't play the chip directly at the hole; instead, he was forced to pitch the ball into a bank on the green 20 feet above the hole and let it trickle back. If he hit it perfectly, he'd be set up for a fairly simple putt for par. But Woods went beyond perfect, and as the ball ambled down the slope toward the cup, it paused for a long, long moment on the lip, its Nike logo winking at the television camera, before dropping for one of the most improbable birdies in Masters history. Woods won his fourth Green Jacket in a playoff against Chris DiMarco.

Something to Jump About

April 11, 2004
Phil Mickelson

For his entire 12-year career, Phil Mickelson was the happy guy the galleries counted on to lose the big ones. But before the 2004 Masters, Mickelson ditched his big-swing short game for a simpler approach preached by guru Dave Pelz. The new strategy worked. After holing an 18-foot birdie putt on the 72nd hole to win his first major, Phil took flight—sort of—in the most ungainly victory leap in sports history.

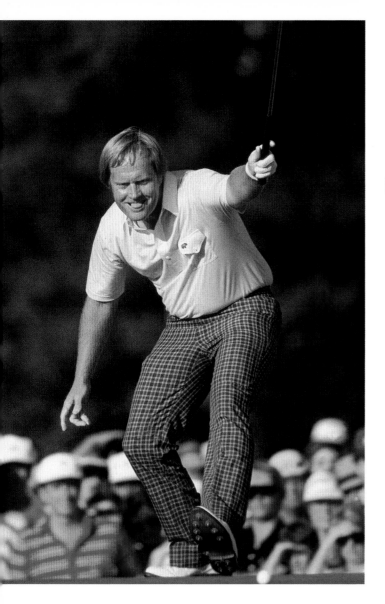

The Bear Maximum

April 13, 1986
Jack Nicklaus

Four shots behind with four holes to play in the Masters, Jack Nicklaus eagled Augusta National's 15th and birdied the 16th. When he holed an 11-footer for birdie at the 17th, he jabbed the air with his putter and stuck his tongue out in delight. The putt capped a back-nine 30 (six under) and a round of 65 that gave Nicklaus, at 46 more Olden Bear than Golden Bear, his sixth Green Jacket and 18th (and final) major championship. Said runner-up Tom Kite: "Even Jack will probably say he's past his prime." Said Nicklaus: "I've been saying that for years." His prime just lasted longer than most.

A Family Affair

April 13, 1997
Tiger Woods

Everyone knew he was coming. Tiger Woods had won three consecutive U.S. Amateur titles and had been raised to be a champion golfer by his father, Earl, a Vietnam vet with a singular vision of what it took to challenge for the title of Best Who Ever Lived. No single shot stood out in Tiger's first Masters victory—when you win by a record 12 shots and beat the best score of six-time champion Jack Nicklaus by a shot, they're all great shots. The moment that did stand out in Woods' victory came after he holed the final putt, walked over to Earl, and gave him a great big teary-eyed hug. Ten major titles later, after Tiger won the 2006 British Open, there were more tears, only this time they were driven by grief, not joy. Just short of three months earlier, on May 3, Earl Woods died after his long struggle with cancer.

A Fine Mess-ier

April 14, 1991
Theo Fleury

With the chance to eliminate Calgary from the playoffs in overtime, Edmonton's Mark Messier made an uncharacteristic mental mistake, sliding a cross-ice pass in front of the star Flames forward Theo Fleury. Calgary's leading scorer picked off the pass and went in unchallenged at Grant Fuhr, easily sneaking the puck through the goalie's legs for a 2-1 win, and tying the series at 3-3. "What can I say?" Messier said. "Give Calgary credit. They were alert and aggressive all through the game. These things happen. All that bothers me is that we could have won and let them off the hook. Let's hope we don't live to regret it." They didn't, but it took a 5-4 win in OT in the seventh game to get Messier off the hook.

Toothless Shark

April 14, 1996
Greg Norman

After years of coming ever so close to winning the Masters, Greg Norman looked like a lock to do it—*finally*. You take a six-stroke lead into the final round at Augusta, you can be excused for daydreaming about what goes best with green. The misery of his final round 78 was highlighted at the 15th hole when a chip that seemed destined to drop for eagle stayed out. Instead, Norman dropped. Nick Faldo blew by him with a 67 to win by five. If you're scoring at home, that's an *11-shot* swing in 18 holes. "I'm disappointed," understated Norman afterward, "but I'm not going to run around and be like Dennis Rodman and head-butt an official." Anyone checked for cracked plaster in the Augusta locker room?

Bull Market

April 16, 1996
Bulls vs. Bucks

It was as near a perfect season as a basketball team has ever had. In the end, the Bulls would finish 72-10 and win the title, but on this night they put the mark in the book that says Best Team of All Time. With an 86-80 win over the Bucks, the Bulls notched their 70th win of the 82-game season, surpassing the mark of 69-13 set by the 1971-72 Lakers. "I'm glad it's over with," said Michael Jordan, who finished with 22 points. "We didn't start out the season to win 70 games. We started out the season to win the championship, and that's still our motivation." The Bulls were pushed along by the Milwaukee crowd of 18,633, which was a sellout in more ways than one. Said Milwaukee coach Mike Dunleavy: "It can be a little disheartening when you have almost as many people cheering for the opposing team."

30,000 for Erving

April 17, 1987
Julius Erving

Dr. J reached yet another milestone with his customary style, grace, and sense of the moment. Playing in the final regular-season home game of his 16-year career, Erving needed 36 points to become just the third player in basketball history to reach 30,000. A tall order for anyone, not to mention a 37-year-old playing on gimpy knees. He did the trick with five minutes still remaining in the third period. Only Karl Malone and Michael Jordan have joined the exclusive club since Erving's retirement, leaving Dr. J No. 5 on the all-time list.

Taking It All in Stride

April 18, 1983
Joan Benoit

She ran so fast so early that a guy running in the race yelled out to Joan Benoit, "Lady, you better watch it!" Then almost all the guys watched the back of her shoes as she tore away, winning the women's division of the Boston Marathon in 2:22:42, or 167 seconds faster than any woman had ever run 26 miles, 385 yards. Benoit's nearest rival was almost seven minutes behind her. If that isn't fast enough for you, consider that since 1946, 10 *male* winners of the Boston Marathon have had slower times than Benoit's.

Duck and Cover

April 19, 2000
Orel Hershiser

The normally unflappable Orel Hershiser was having the kind of game Bob Uecker should have been calling in his "Harry Doyle" voice, from *Major League*. LA's Hershiser tied a major-league mark by hitting four batters in a single game, and he did it in just 1⅓ innings. On the receiving end of the worst of it was Houston's Richard Hidalgo, who got plunked twice by Hershiser and then again by reliever Matt Herges. Hidalgo's three bruises also tied a record. "I'm not sure if I want that record" Hidalgo said. "Man, I'm sore. I've never seen anyone that wild before."

Dinger Derby

April 19, 2005
Mets vs. Phillies

The good people of Philadelphia must have wondered if it was hailing baseballs. In a 16-4 rout of the homeboy Phils, the Mets unleashed a club record seven dingers: one each from Doug Mientkiewicz and Mike Piazza (a 471-foot blast that nearly reached the outfield concourse), two each from Victor Diaz and Jose Reyes, and then the capper, a granny from third baseman David Wright. On his next at-bat, Wright nearly made it eight big flies on the day, but came up a few feet shy. "I just felt like every swing the ball was going out," said Wright. And he was almost right.

How He Played the Game

April 20, 1986
Michael Jordan

If his team wasn't up to the task of facing Larry Bird and Boston, then Michael Jordan surely was. Playing 53 of 58 minutes of a double-overtime game in the first round of the playoffs, MJ hit 22-of-41 from the field and took the rest of his 63 total points from the line. But in the end it wasn't enough, as Chicago fell 135-131. "I think he's God disguised as Michael Jordan," said Bird, who scored 36 points. "He put on one of the greatest shows of all time."

Sleight of Foot

April 21, 1980
Rosie Ruiz

Six months after placing a strong 24th in the New York Marathon, Cuban runner Rosie Ruiz won the Boston Marathon. After being awarded the laurel wreath for her then-record time of 2:31:56, Ruiz said, "I just wanted to finish, because at the 13th or 14th mile I felt I was going to collapse. To be sincere, this is a dream." Yep, it sure was a dream. Ruiz had jumped out of the crowd and rejoined the race somewhere near the finish. There were immediate claims of fraud, and they were confirmed in the following days, along with the fact that her time in the New York Marathon was also suspect; at least one New Yorker claimed to have seen Ruiz riding the subway on her way to the front of the pack.

Caminiti for the Defense

April 22, 1996
Ken Caminiti

Ken Caminiti might have won his second consecutive Gold Glove with this single play in April. Certainly Gold Glove voters saw his effort, which won an ESPY for Baseball Play of the Year, replayed often enough. The diving backhanded stop of the Marlins' Greg Colbrunn's hot shot was special; the throw, from a seated position on the foul line behind third, was spectacular. And it was a good omen for the rest of the season—after batting .326, with 40 home runs and 130 RBIs, Caminiti earned the NL MVP Award and helped bring home a division title for the Padres.

One Slamming Inning

April 23, 1999
Fernando Tatis

Chan Ho Park would see better days. The Dodgers hurler was facing
Fernando Tatis with the bases loaded in the third and no one out. On the
surface, no big deal. The Cardinals' third baseman had only homered 23
times in his two-plus seasons in the bigs. But Tatis took Park deep for a
granny. *Ouch!* And then, a little later in the same inning, he did it to him
again. *Ouch! Ouch!* No other player in major league history had ever hit
two grand slams in a single stanza, nor had anybody driven in eight runs
in the same frame. And Park? He could take solace in the fact that he had
helped make history.

Baring It All

April 26, 1989
Kevin Mitchell

In an early-season game, the first-place Giants lost to St. Louis, 3-1. Ho-hum. But what had people humming after the game was the catch SF outfielder Kevin Mitchell made on an Ozzie Smith drive that was curving foul. As Mitchell humped it toward the line he overran the ball, then at the last second reached back and caught it with his bare hand. Admiring the play later, Giants pitcher Kelly Downs said, "That'll be on highlight reels for the next 50 years." Well, at least 17.

Precision Rocket Strikes

April 29, 1986
Roger Clemens

There are, the rulebook tells us, 27 outs per side in a standard, nine-inning baseball game, and before this night the most any pitcher had ever struck out in such a contest was 19, a record shared by three gods of the mound: Steve Carlton, Tom Seaver, and Nolan Ryan. In a 3-1 Red Sox win over the Mariners, Roger Clemens sat down 20, including eight in a row during the fourth, fifth, and sixth innings. "The strikeouts just kept on coming," Clemens said after the game. "I knew something was happening because of the way the fans were reacting." Something, indeed: Clemens threw 97 strikes in 138 pitches, walked no one, and gave up just three hits on his way into the record book.

On the Flip Side

April 29, 2006
Tony Stewart

Tony Stewart loves to race so much that he'd put wheels on a washing machine if that's what it took. And just because he's one of the big boys doesn't mean he passes up those Busch races. At the Aaron's 312 Buschy at Talladega, Stewart was the on-again, off-again leader until lap 67, when a little contact sent him sliding around in the grass. His car flipped, going airborne for a good long while before skidding, wheels-up, down almost a quarter-mile of racetrack. Stewart walked away unharmed.

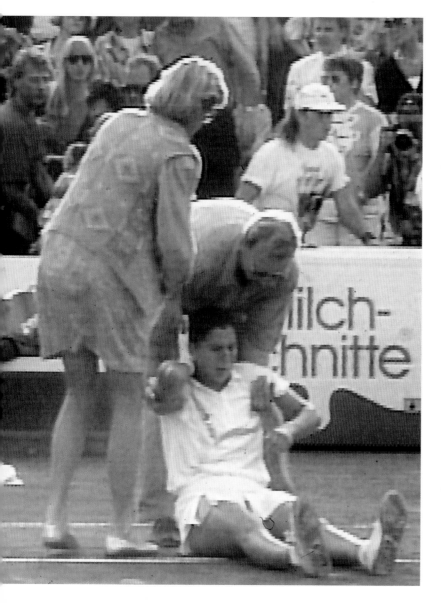

Wounded in Service

April 30, 1993
Monica Seles

"Fan" is short for "fanatic," as every sports nut knows, but the moniker reached an ugly new low when a mentally disturbed German fan of Steffi Graf's—then the No. 2-ranked player in the world—leaned over from the stands and slashed No. 1 Monica Seles during a match in Hamburg. The wound healed quickly; the emotional damage, not so fast. Seles did rejoin the circuit in the summer of 1995 and grabbed the Australian Open title a final time in January of 1996.

May

Grand Larceny

May 1, 1991
Rickey Henderson

With this snatching of third base, Oakland's Rickey Henderson became the all-time stolen base leader with 939, one more than Lou Brock. Henderson's thievery to that point added up to some 16 miles of illicit baserunning over a little more than 12 seasons. "Lou Brock was the symbol of great base stealing," the always self-effacing Henderson proclaimed afterward, "but today I'm the greatest of all time."

Going ... Going ... Not Gone

May 2, 2005
Ichiro Suzuki

The Angels were clubbing the Mariners at Safeco Field, but it would have been even worse if Ichiro Suzuki hadn't made a "Did you see what I just saw?" outfield play. Angels slugger Garret Anderson launched a long drive to rightfield, a homer for certain, except that Anderson was out before he got to second. Huh? See, Ichiro raced back, sprang off the warning track, dug his cleat into the padding on the wall, vaulted up and over the rail, and reached back to catch Anderson's drive. "I imagined the ball to be hit a little farther than it was," Ichiro said later through an interpreter. "When I got up there, it looked like a basketball." Score it a blocked shot.

Senior Moment

May 3, 1986
Bill Shoemaker

Just three weeks after Jack Nicklaus, 46, won the Masters (*see* April 13, 1986), Bill Shoemaker, 54, rode 17-to-1 shot Ferdinand to victory in the Kentucky Derby. It was The Shoe's fourth Derby crown, and he did it on a horse that was dead last at the half-mile point and fourth as the field started down the stretch. "I had a choice of going around those three horses or going through the hole," Shoemaker said. "But the rail is always the shortest way home and a couple of horses on the rail looked like they were stopping, so I decided to shoot through that hole."

Outta Here?
No, Up There!

May 4, 1984
Dave Kingman

The long, towering fly ball was Dave Kingman's trademark throughout his career, and the A's designated hitter was at the top of his slugging form when Oakland paid a visit to the Twins in the Metrodome. In the fourth inning, Kingman took a typically huge cut at a Frank Viola offering and sent it up, up, up ... but it never came down, down, down. The ball had slipped inside the fabric of the dome's ceiling, 186 feet above the playing surface. The umpires awarded Kingman a ground-rule double.

Business as Usual

May 5, 1981

Larry Bird

Just another quintessential Bird play: fast, smart, game-changing. Nothing out of the ordinary—for him. In Game 1 of the NBA Finals against the Houston Rockets, Larry Bird put up a simple jumper that bounced off the rim. Hey, even superstars miss now and again. By the time the ball reversed direction, though, Bird was already on his way to the right baseline, where he grabbed his own rebound, transferred the ball from his right to left hand, and kissed a shot off the glass while falling out of bounds. The Celtics would win the Finals in six.

The Old One-Two

May 5, 1993
Greg Maddux

You're Greg Maddux. You're known for your slider, not for your foot speed. But you're on second base, not the mound, so when a Braves teammate hits one up the middle, you chug dutifully toward home. One problem: the Pirates' catcher, Don Slaught, is waiting for you 10 feet up the third baseline, whistling a tune to kill time as you approach the plate. You know you're dead, so you jump over the tag. Yes! *No!* Whoops! You miss the plate on the other side. When Slaught notices the ump hasn't made a call, he comes for you. You juke left, he bites, and you zig right and score. "The thing was," Maddux said later, "I came to the plate and I wasn't ready to slide and I wasn't ready to run him over. So I leaped. Then I thought about walking off, thinking maybe they thought I touched the plate. But Slaught came after me, so I made the move. I really don't know where that move came from."

Reggie 8, Knicks 0

May 7, 1995
Reggie Miller

The Indiana Pacers trailed the New York Knicks by six with just 18.7 seconds to go in Game 1 of the Eastern Conference semifinals. "Realistically, I thought we had no chance," Pacers coach Larry Brown said later, "but I ain't going to tell them that." For certain, he didn't tell Reggie Miller, who drained a three with 16.4 seconds left in the game. On the ensuing inbounds play, New York's Anthony Mason fretted over being called for a five-second violation, but couldn't call a timeout because the Knicks were fresh out. In desperation, Mason floated a pass to Greg Anthony, who stumbled with some help from Miller, who then intercepted the pass. Instead of driving for a layup, Miller calmly dribbled back outside the arc and popped another three. The plot thickened when Indy's Sam Mitchell, thinking his team still trailed, fouled John Starks on the inbounds play. (Dude, check the scoreboard.) Starks clanked iron on both free throws, but Knicks center Patrick Ewing hauled in the rebound on the second miss, only to miss his own close-range shot. The rebound off of Ewing's miss was gobbled up by Miller, who was fouled by Mason in the process. Reggie made his two charity shots, bringing his 11-second total to 8 points. The Pacers won 107-105.

Hammer Time

May 7, 2005
Diego Corrales vs. Jose Luis Castillo

For nine rounds, lightweights Diego Corrales and Jose Luis Castillo beat on each other relentlessly in brutal, toe-to-toe combat. In the 10th, Corrales teetered on the brink of oblivion, going down twice under ferocious left hooks from Castillo. Corrales staggered to his feet after the second knockdown, the battered, unsteady poster image of a TKO waiting to happen. But when the fight resumed, Corrales maniacally attacked, landing a killer left hook to Castillo's face to begin a quick four-punch flurry that threw the fight into reverse and nearly removed Castillo's head from his neck. Mercifully, the ref stepped in and called the fight. Corrales won by TKO. Afterward, Corrales' trainer, Joe Goosen, said, "You'd have to be sadistic to want to see this again."

The Mightiest Duck

May 10, 2003
Jean-Sebastien Giguere

The Mighty Ducks eventually beat the Minnesota Wild 1-0 in double OT in the first game of the Western Conference finals, but the marathon battle would have never made it into extra periods without a show-stopping save by Jean-Sebastien Giguere, who turned away 39 Wild shots on the night. The highlight thrill came on a power play in the second period, when it seemed as if Marian Gaborik had an open look at a backhander in front of the net. Giguere threw his body back toward the line and stopped the puck with the blade of his stick. "A little bit lucky for me," Giguere said. "Just kind of a diving save. Sometimes you need one of those." Plus 38 "routine" ones.

Take One for the Team

May 11, 2006
Aaron Rowand

It was a dark and stormy night, and the Phillies beat the Mets 2-0 in a rain-shortened four-and-a-half-inning affair. But the Phils might have lost the mini-game if not for one play. With the bases loaded and two outs in the first, New York's Xavier Nady drove a ball to the warning track in centerfield, only to watch as Philly's Aaron Rowand made a superb one-handed, over-the-shoulder, plowing-into-the-fence catch to save at least three runs. Only hitch: Rowand's face-off with Citizens Bank Park broke his nose and sent him straight to the 15-day DL.

Too Gooden

May 14, 1996
Dwight Gooden

Problems with drugs had forced Dwight Gooden out of the game entirely for the better part of two years, and when he signed on with the Yankees in 1996, there was no realistic expectation that the wizardry he'd exhibited in leading the Mets to victory in the 1986 World Series was still in his repertoire. Just a few weeks earlier, the Yanks had relegated Gooden to the bullpen and considered sending him down to the minors. But in his seventh start for the Pinstripers, Gooden struck out five, walked six, and allowed no one to reach first on a batted ball in a 2-0 no-hit win over Seattle. "This is the greatest feeling," said Gooden. "In my wildest dreams I never could have imagined this. This is sweet."

Sure Cure for Boredom

May 15, 2004
Roy Jones Jr. vs. Antonio Tarver

Roy Jones Jr. brought a 49-1 record into the ring, but he evidently forgot to show his résumé to opponent Antonio Tarver. Jones, who'd never been seriously rocked in a professional bout, was knocked goofy by a single punch at 1:41 into the second round. The hard left, one of the first punches Tarver threw in the fight, sent Jones halfway through the ropes and rendered him incapable of regaining solid footing before the ref stopped the fight. "He missed with the right and I turned it over right after he did with an overhand left, right on the kisser," said Tarver, who regained the WBC light heavyweight crown he'd lost to Jones by decision the year before. "It was beautiful." That's not the way Jones saw it: "I was dictating the fight, but I got bored with it. This fight was really nothing to me." At least it was short.

Front and Center

May 16, 1980
Magic Johnson

They trailed the Lakers 3-2 in the NBA Finals, but the Sixers had good reason to believe they'd draw even in Game 6. For starters, the game was at home in Philly. And for non-starters, Kareem Abdul-Jabbar would sit the game out with an ankle injury. That meant Philly would dominate in the paint, which ... Stop right there. What actually happened is that a 6'8" rookie guard named Magic Johnson took over at center for the Lakers—and took over the game. Johnson scored 42 points, 15 rebounds, and 7 assists in a 123-107 cakewalk on his way to winning the series MVP Award. "The trouble for the 76ers tonight was Magic," said Lakers coach Paul Westhead. "Our Magical Man, our Houdini. Who would have thought we could win in Philadelphia without Kareem and with Magic playing center?"

The Long Bounce

May 16, 1999
Allan Houston

Allan Houston's final-second shot in Game 5 of the Eastern Conference semifinals between the Knicks and the Heat bounced hard off the rim, and for a couple of long heartbeats no one could tell if it would drop. It hung in the air so long, everyone watching could recall the events leading up to the bounce: a near-steal by the Heat's Terry Porter with 4.5 seconds remaining; a quick inbound to Houston; then a fast drive and a one-handed running jumper from 14 feet out. And then it dropped, with .8 seconds left on the clock, putting the Knicks up 78-77. The Heat's last-gasp 40-footer was a miss, and the Knicks took the semis, three games to two.

The "Pass in the Grass" that Wasn't

May 17, 1987
Dale Earnhardt vs. Bill Elliott

Once and for all, let's get something straight: Dale Earnhardt *already had the lead* when his No. 3 car made contact with Bill Elliott's ride on the backstretch at the Charlotte Motor Speedway during The All-Star Challenge (a.k.a The Winston). The Intimidator *then* mowed the infield grass while *holding* the lead on his way to the first of his three All-Star wins. *Not a pass* in the grass, okay? A *hold* in the grass. Are we clear on that? Thank you for your attention.

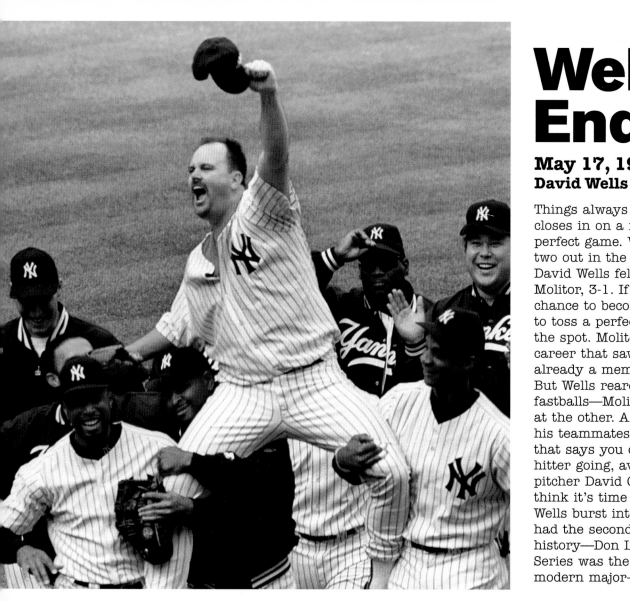

Wells Ends Well

May 17, 1998
David Wells

Things always get a little hairy as a pitcher closes in on a no-hitter, never mind a perfect game. With a perfecto going with two out in the seventh, Yankees' lefty David Wells fell behind Minnesota's Paul Molitor, 3-1. If Wells was going to blow his chance to become just the second Yankee to toss a perfect game, this looked like the spot. Molitor, in the last season of a career that saw him hit .306 lifetime, was already a member of the 3,000 Hit Club. But Wells reared back and threw two perfect fastballs—Molitor looked at one and waved at the other. As Wells headed to the dugout, his teammates, following the unwritten rule that says you don't talk to a guy with a no-hitter going, avoided him. All except veteran pitcher David Cone, who said to Wells, "I think it's time to break out the knuckleball." Wells burst into laughter. Six outs later, Wells had the second perfect game in Yankees history—Don Larsen's in the 1956 World Series was the first—and just the 13th in modern major-league history.

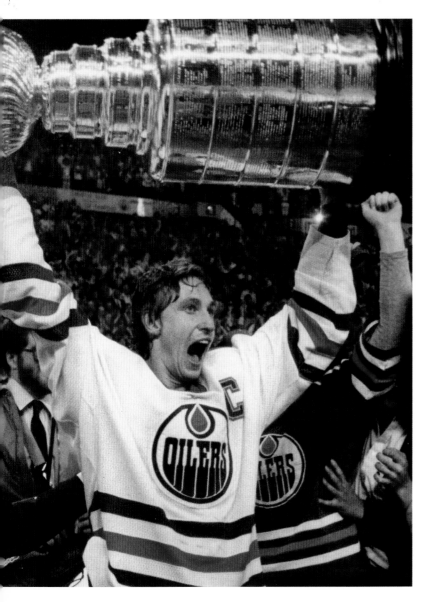

The Great One Delivers

May 19, 1984
Edmonton Oilers

After providing a home for Lord Stanley's Cup for four straight years, the New York Islanders surrendered the trophy to the next dynasty, the Edmonton Oilers of Wayne Gretzky and Mark Messier. Up 3-1 entering Game 5, the Oilers erased the sting of a four-game sweep at the hands of the Islanders the year before. "We couldn't stop the wave," said Isles coach Al Arbour of the overwhelming talent his team faced. In the final game, it was Gretzky's two goals and one assist that posted the Oilers to a 4-0 lead on the way to an easy 5-2 victory.

Silence Reigns

May 20, 1989
Sunday Silence vs. Easy Goer

And down the stretch they came! In one of the closest Preakness Stakes ever run, Sunday Silence, a black colt from California, came from behind to edge out Easy Goer by a nose. Not so easygoing? Pat Day, Easy's rider, subsequently claimed he was fouled in the run for the wire. His protest was rejected and the result stood. Silence was golden.

The Tide Slide

May 21, 1989
Rusty Wallace vs. Darrell Waltrip

With just over two miles remaining at The Winston, Rusty Wallace found Darrell Waltrip's back panel a temptation too luscious to resist. A little tap in the fourth corner at Charlotte Motor Speedway sent Waltrip spinning. The yellow flag came out and sent Waltrip to the back of the lead lap—over his strenuous objections—and left Wallace out in front, where he'd soon win. The love tap didn't go down well with the Tide car's crew, who gathered to greet Wallace on the way to Winner's Circle. Waltrip called the foul flagrant, but Wallace dismissed him, saying, "If a man thinks this is a leisurely Sunday afternoon ride, he ought not to be in the race."

Just One of the Guys

May 22, 2003
Annika Sorenstam

As the first woman to play in a PGA Tour event since Babe Zaharias, Annika Sorenstam didn't waste much time getting the crowd behind her at the Colonial in Fort Worth. On her fourth hole, a 178-yard par 3, she took a 6-iron right over the flag, leaving it just off the back of the green, 15 slick feet from birdie. Leaving the pin in, Sorenstam coaxed the ball gently toward the hole and watched it tumble for birdie. The crowd exploded in cheers, and although she eventually missed the cut, her first-round 71 left her ahead of 27 PGA Tour players.

Money Talks, Losers Walk

May 24, 2003
Chris Moneymaker

The annals of "You Can't Make This Stuff Up" might have a new chapter. From absolute neophyte to the top poker player in the world in three years? From playing online to sitting across from and staring down the legendary champions of the game? From the $40 entry fee for the online tournament that qualified him to a $2.5 million prize? And what was that name again? Ah, yes, Moneymaker. Chris Moneymaker. The showdown between the 27-year-old accountant and poker poobah Sam Farha capped five weeks of nonstop action at the World Series of Poker. While Moneymaker conceded that he got away with many a bluff during the tournament, the final hand was sheer good fortune. Farha went all in with a pair of jacks after the flop. Smart play, except for one thing: the lowly four and five on the flop matched Moneymaker's hole cards. Another five on the river gave Moneymaker a triumphant full house—and $2.5 million.

Starks to the Rack

May 25, 1993
John Starks

It was an astonishing play, a soaring left-handed dunk from the right baseline. Most astonishing, in a reversal approaching an alternative reality, its author was John Starks, and the defender too late to stop it was Michael Jordan. The dunk, coming with less than a minute left to help seal a 96-91 victory and a 2-0 series lead for the Knicks in the Eastern Conference finals, raised New York hopes that the Knicks were on the way to dethroning the two-time defending champion Bulls. But though the replayed dunk would pump up many a future Garden crowd, it would be the high point of the series for New York. Eight days later, back at the Garden with the series now tied at 2-2, another sequence under and above the basket would doom the Knicks' quest: four in-close attempts by Charles Smith in the closing seconds were denied. The Bulls prevailed in Chicago in Game 6.

Cut Down the Nets

May 25, 2002
Celtics vs. Nets

When you lead by 21 to start the fourth quarter of an NBA playoff game, like the Nets did in Game 3 of the Eastern Conference finals, and you have Jason Kidd on the floor to help you control the tempo of the game, like the Nets did, the win should be money in the bank. Except in this case the bank was robbed by Paul Pierce's 19 final-period points, which led Boston to a 94-90 win. It was the biggest fourth-quarter comeback in playoff history. "You kind of see it in their eyes," Pierce said afterward. "It didn't seem like anybody wanted to shoot the ball for them. As we got closer to them, as we got more aggressive, as we started feeding off the crowd." No Kidd-ing.

The Way the Ball Bounces

May 26, 1993
Jose Canseco

If there's a test in every man's life to determine his ability to laugh at himself, Jose Canseco passed his with flying colors. Accustomed to inspiring awe with tape-measure homers, Canseco provided comic relief with an unusual assist to Indians batter Carlos Martinez's fourth-inning fly ball. Battling the lights and groping for the wall, Canseco staggered helplessly as the ball bounced off his head and over the fence. He initially signaled that the ball hit his outstretched glove, but no one was buying it.

Blown Call

May 27, 1981
Lenny Randle

Kansas City's Amos Otis, always a tough out, was never tougher than on this at-bat against the Mariners. When Otis barely nipped a pitch that trickled down the third baseline, three Mariners, including third bagger Lenny Randle, moved toward the ball. Randle saw at once that it was moving too slow for Randle to make a play on Otis at first and that his only hope was for the ball to roll foul. Randle had a brainstorm: why not give it a helping hand? Or blow? So Randle dropped to all fours and huffed and puffed to blow the ball foul. The home plate ump initially called the ball foul, but after KC manager Jim Frey let loose some wind of his own, Otis was awarded first. Randle was perplexed. "I didn't blow it," Randle said. "I used the power of suggestion. I yelled at it, 'Go foul, go foul.'"

Don't Fence Him In

May 27, 1991
Rodney McCray

Many a player has said he'd run through a wall for his manager. Only outfielder Rodney McCray, playing for Marv Foley's AAA Vancouver Canadians, can say he's actually done it. McCray's headlong rush through the plywood fence at Civic Stadium in Portland yielded little. He didn't make the catch and the advertising now immortalized in blooper films is strictly local. "I just wish I had run through something like a Coca-Cola sign so I could have gotten some endorsements," McCray lamented. Fifteen years later, he caught a glimmer of commercial hope: the Portland Beavers commemorated his non-catch with a Rodney McCray Bobblefence Night.

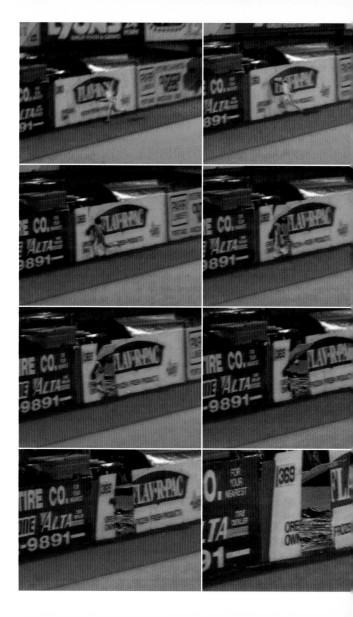

Mission Impossible

May 28, 2000
Shaquille O'Neal

The most amazing thing about the Lakers' 103-91 win over Portland in Game 4 of the Western Conference finals was not that they once trailed by 11. Nor was it that this was the Blazers' second straight loss at home, where they hardly ever lost. No, the really astonishing thing was this: when Portland went to the money strategy of putting Shaq—an infamous bricklayer from the charity stripe—on the line for his guaranteed misses, the big guy stunned not just the Western Conference but the Western World by going 9-for-9, including 6-for-6 in the fourth quarter. "Excuse me, excuse me," O'Neal said as he plowed through reporters in the locker room after the game. "The Big Maravich coming through."

Follow Her Lead

May 29, 2005
Danica Patrick

When 23-year-old Danica Patrick flashed into the lead with 10 laps to go in the Indy 500, she became the first woman ever to lead the fabled race. In the end, a fuel shortage did her in. Her team's boss decided to gamble that she could make it to the checkered flag without a final pit stop, but trying to get the fuel mix just right caused Patrick to slow down, and she was passed with six laps left by Dan Wheldon, who held on to win. Patrick finished fourth, but wasn't buying all the "great job for a woman" stuff after the race. "Are you kidding me?" said Patrick, in response to a reporter's question after the race. "I made a hell of a point for *anybody*."

Too Close for Comfort

May 30, 1982
Gordon Johncock

With his car handling like a dump truck (albeit a dump truck averaging 162.029 mph) and Rick Mears cutting 12 seconds off his lead in the final 13 laps, Gordon Johncock crossed the Indy 500 finish line 16-hundredths of a second—about half a car length—in front of Mears in the closest Indy ever. "One more lap," Mears said, "and it could have been 16-hundredths of a second the other way." When somebody suggested that agonized fans might not have been able to endure that one more lap, Johncock said, "I don't think I could, either."

Queen of the Hill

May 31, 1997
Ila Borders

When Ila Borders entered the game in relief in the sixth inning for the St. Paul Saints of the Northern League, she became—thanks to an inspired move by team owner-ringmaster Mike Veeck—the first woman to pitch in a regular-season game in minor league baseball. Alas, things didn't go exactly as the lefty hoped. She hit the first batter, balked in a runner from third facing her second batter, then knocked down a line drive and threw wildly to first for an error. That wasn't quite enough to get her the hook, but an RBI double by the next hitter was. "That's going to haunt me for the rest of my life," Borders said. "I don't think you're ever going to bounce back from that." But she did just that. The next day, Borders struck out the side.

Walk the Line

May 31, 1999
Sean Elliott

With nine seconds left in Game 2 of the
Western Conference finals and the Spurs
trailing the Blazers 85-83, Sean Elliott took
an inbounds pass and nearly fell out of
bounds. Wobbling, he managed to stay in just
long enough to launch a desperate heave
over the onrushing arms of Rasheed Wallace.
Nothing but net! As it was Elliott's sixth trey
of the night, it would be caddish to suggest
that pure, blind luck had anything to do with
the result. "When I caught it, I thought I was
going to fall out of bounds," Elliott said. "My
jumper felt good all day so I just wanted to
get an attempt at it. I just wanted to get the
shot up." And down.

June

Loose Cannon

June 1, 2004
Milton Bradley

Dodgers outfielder Milton Bradley always had a rep for being a bit of a loose cannon, but even he was a little surprised to get tossed from the game as he entered the batter's box to begin a sixth-inning at-bat against Milwaukee. Bradley was busy jawing at the home plate ump, Terry Craft, about previous calls (in at-bats extending nobody knows how far back) when he got the heave-ho. Fearing the worst, LA manager Jim Tracy raced out to restrain Bradley, who then took off his batting gloves and helmet and left them at the plate, along with his bat. But Bradley was just getting warmed up. Back in the dugout, he picked up a bag of balls and threw it onto the field. Then he picked up a ball and fired it into the outfield. The outcome? A four-game suspension. "He attempted to embarrass the umpires," said ump crew chief Joe West. Good call, Joe.

Just Don't Get Her Mad

June 2, 1985
Nancy Lopez

Nancy Lopez was within reach of tying or even breaking Patty Sheehan's course record of 63 during the first round of the LPGA Championship in Mason, Ohio, when officials hit her with a two-stroke penalty for slow play on her next-to-last hole of the round. Fighting back tears of frustration, she birdied her final hole of the day, ending the round with a 65. Lopez was still upset going into Sunday's final round, tied for first with Alice Miller. But she decided she wanted to win the championship, penalties be damned. "I was able to make that madness make me more determined," she said. She played some of the most precise golf of her career, while Miller slumped. Lopez carded three birdies on her first nine holes and coasted to her second LPGA Championship, eight shots ahead of Miller.

Go Down, Moses

June 4, 1987
Edwin Moses

For 122 consecutive races, spread over almost 10 years, Edwin Moses had been invincible in the 400-meter hurdles. Track fans had come to believe that no one could beat him. Then, in an early summer meet in Madrid on the European swing, someone did. A 21-year-old American named Danny Harris, who had placed second to Moses in the 1984 Olympics, nipped the champ by .13 seconds. "I ran a good race," Moses told the press afterward, "and the guy that beat me is 10 years younger and ran the race of his life." Harris' ascendancy didn't last long: later that summer, in a rematch at the World Championships in Rome, Moses edged him by .02 seconds.

Battle Cry

June 4, 2003
Tim Duncan

He was quiet during the first half against the Nets, but when Game 1 of the NBA Finals was on the line, San Antonio's Tim Duncan roared to life—literally. Four minutes into the fourth quarter, Duncan slammed home a hard dunk over Aaron Williams and let out a war whoop. Observers found the cry way out of character for the hardworking MVP, but Duncan disagreed when asked about it after the game. "I don't know if I played any different," he said. "What's not to be excited about?" Unstoppable down low, and even draining jump shots, Duncan scored 24 on 8-for-10 shooting from the field in the second half. He finished the night with 32 points. "When Tim starts hitting jump shots from 17 feet," said Nets coach Byron Scott, "then you're in trouble." Big trouble.

American *Fútbol*

June 5, 2002
U.S. Soccer

The American team hadn't won a World Cup game outside their own country since 1950. Now, 52 years later in South Korea, they were paired against the mighty Portuguese team in the opening round. America's chances of beating a team ranked No. 5 in the world? Somewhere between none and none. But time stood still, water ran uphill, pigs flew—and the USA, after jumping out to a 3-0 lead, held on to win 3-2. The U.S. scored its three goals in the first 36 minutes, including a lucky deflection when a cross by Landon Donovan nicked off a defender and went into the net. Donovan was stunned, and so were the bookies: one U.K. betting house reduced the odds against Team USA's winning the World Cup from 300:1 to 100:1. It was not to be. The Americans did beat Mexico 2-0 in the Round of 16—a minor miracle itself—but lost to Germany 1-0 in the quarterfinals.

Out of Nowhere

June 5, 2004
Smarty Jones vs. Birdstone

Sentimental favorite Smarty Jones, winner of the Kentucky Derby and the Preakness, had 120,000 people jammed into Belmont Park (and millions more glued to TV screens) hoping to see the first Triple Crown winner since Affirmed in 1978. And with a half-mile to go and Smarty holding a four-length lead, everyone figured the unlikely horse from Philadelphia had it won. Everyone, that is, but Birdstone, the 36-to-1 underdog, and his jockey, Edgar Prado. Gobbling up ground as the horses rounded the far turn, Birdstone nosed ahead halfway down the home stretch. Stewart Elliott, Smarty's rider, asked his horse for a final surge, but it wasn't to be. At the finish, it was Birdstone by a length. "He ran and he ran," Elliott said of Smarty Jones. "That horse just came and ran us down."

One and Done

June 7, 1995
Rockets vs. Magic

Game 1 in the NBA Finals typically sets a tone or a theme for the series but can't—or shouldn't—determine the outcome. This one did. With his team leading the Rockets by three, Magic guard Nick Anderson missed four free throws during the final 10.5 seconds of the game, leaving the door ajar for the Rockets' Kenny Smith to drop a trey with 1.6 seconds left in regulation that knotted the game. In overtime, Hakeem Olajuwon gave the Rockets the victory by tipping in a rebound off a Clyde Drexler miss. The loss sucked the life out of Orlando. Houston went on to crush the Magic in four straight games.

Save Your Best

June 8, 1996
Warren Morris

LSU second baseman Warren Morris had missed 40 games after busting his right hand in April, and in the games he did play, he hadn't hit a single home run. Yet his team was 21-0 with him in the lineup, and with two outs in the bottom of the ninth and LSU trailing Miami 8-7, Morris kept that undefeated streak alive. With one man on, Morris smashed a pitch from Canes freshman Robbie Morrison that just cleared the rightfield fence to give LSU its third College World Series title in six years.

Say, That Guy Looks Familiar

June 9, 1999
Bobby Valentine

In the long tradition of managers who've been ejected from games, Mets skipper Bobby Valentine hung around by the dugout steps to continue issuing orders after he was tossed in the 12th inning of a game against Toronto. Only Valentine, never subtle in his approach to things, went undercover, donning a fake mustache and sunglasses. His disguise didn't fool the TV cameras, however, and when the league office got wind of his prank, he was suspended for two games. His players remained faithful though—they showed up at Shea wearing eyeblack strips as mustaches.

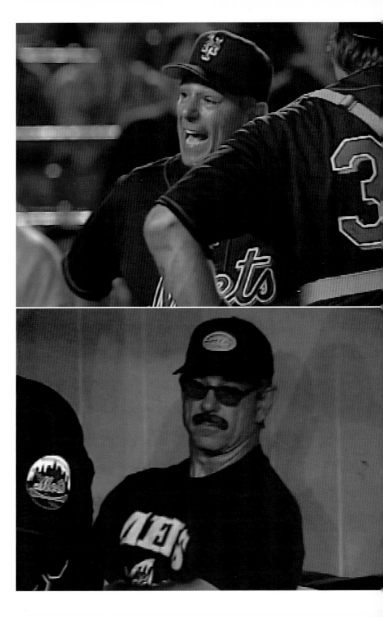

Give Her Another Shot

June 10, 1986
Nancy Lieberman

A woman had never played men's professional basketball before Nancy Lieberman took the floor for the Springfield Fame in a United States Basketball League game against the Staten Island Stallions. The 5'10" Lieberman had earned her historic start by scoring 10 points in a Fame exhibition game. Against the Stallions, she entered the game with 3:40 left in the second quarter and was double-teamed every time she touched the ball. Lieberman never got off a shot and didn't play in the second half, despite chants of "Nan-cy! Nan-cy!" from fans trying to persuade Fame coach Henry Bibby to send her back in. After the game, Lieberman said, "Maybe people will associate me with change and changing attitudes in how the game should be played, without it being wrong to say, 'She plays like a guy.'"

Under the Weather, Head in the Clouds

June 11, 1997
Michael Jordan

You've no doubt had the flu, and you know the best you can do is crawl up on the couch and hide under a blanket until you're strong enough to use the remote to switch from the Home Shopping Network to ESPN. That's how Michael Jordan felt in Game 5 of the NBA Finals against Utah, and yet he scored 38 points while the rest of the Bulls sleepwalked. MJ racked up 15 of his team's 23 points in the fourth quarter, including the ones that put the Bulls in the lead to stay. Final score: Chicago 90, Utah 88. When it was over, the exhausted Jordan was helped from the court by Scottie Pippen. "I didn't even think he was going to be able to put his uniform on," Pippen said. "I wish we could have done more to help him."

Foul Play

June 12, 2001
Yankee Stadium

It was an unusual game for the defending champion New York Yankees. The normally invulnerable Mariano Rivera blew a save by surrendering a home run in the ninth. Then Ramiro Mendoza, about to complete a third perfect inning in the 12th, gave up what everyone thought was a long strike as Expos pinch-hitter Mark Smith's low drive appeared to hook left of the leftfield foul pole. But the umpiring crew caucused and decided the ball was fair. Perhaps they were fooled by the absence of a screen at the bottom of the pole. The three-foot gap between the top of the wall and the bottom of the screen—left clear to prevent any obstruction of fans' view—was filled in the next day.

Lift Your Cups

June 14, 1994
New York Rangers

With a 3-2 win over Vancouver in the NHL Finals, the Mark Messier-led Rangers won the Stanley Cup for the first time since 1940. The series was filled with big plays, but the biggest moment for the 18,200 Rangers fans packed into Madison Square Garden came when Messier skated the Cup around the ice. "They talk about ghosts and dragons," Messier said. "You can't be afraid to slay the dragon."

Big If

June 14, 1998
Michael Jordan

If you're Michael Jordan and you're playing in your last NBA Finals game, you can score six points—your team's only points—in the waning minutes to keep the Bulls in the game. If you're Michael Jordan, you can sneak up on Karl Malone like a thief in the night and steal the ball with 19 seconds remaining and your team trailing 86-85. And if you're Michael Jordan, after that steal you can get away with a gentle shove of Utah's Bryon Russell to create just enough space for you to knock down an 18-footer with 5.2 seconds left, leading the Bulls to an 87-86 win and their sixth NBA title. You can do all that if you're Michael Jordan.

As Easy as One, Two, Three (Times Three)

June 15, 1991
Andy Ashby

He was the losing pitcher in a Phillies-Reds game that Cincy won 3-1. But in the fourth inning, Philadelphia's Andy Ashby did something only 11 pitchers in major league history had done before: he struck out three batters on nine pitches.

Payback in the Big Apple

June 15, 2002
Shawn Estes vs. Roger Clemens

It was inevitable that the Mets were going to retaliate
when Roger Clemens and the Yankees came to Shea for
an interleague game between the two New York teams.
After all, this was Clemens' first at bat against the Mets
since he threw a hunk of bat in Mike Piazza's "general
direction" during the 2000 World Series (see October 22,
2000). So when he batted in the third, the Shea faithful
were screaming for blood and Mets pitcher Shawn Estes
threw a baby softball—87 mph, tops—low and tight and
behind Clemens, just missing the back of his thigh as
Clemens leaned forward. No stranger to the payback
pitch himself, Clemens tipped his batting helmet toward
Estes. He gladly would have taken a hard one in the ribs
to avoid the real ignominy of the day: a few innings later,
Clemens served up a homer to Estes, the first time in
his career The Rocket gave up a dinger to an opposing
pitcher.

White Flag of Victory

June 17, 1984
Fuzzy Zoeller

As he watched from the fairway as Greg Norman rolled in a 50-foot putt on the final hole of the U.S. Open, Fuzzy Zoeller assumed the putt was for a birdie and the victory. So the easygoing Fuzzman did what came naturally—at least to him. He took the big white towel draped across his clubs and waved it in mock surrender. Norman, not knowing quite how to react because his putt was actually for par, waved back. ABC anchor Jim McKay was moved to say, "This is marvelous golf and marvelous sportsmanship, the kind of thing tennis used to be known for." The towel-snapping buddies faced off the next day in an 18-hole playoff, in which Zoeller gutted The Shark by eight shots.

Juice on the Loose

June 17, 1994
O.J. Simpson

Sports fans were anticipating a good TV day: Knicks vs. Rockets in the NBA Finals. Instead, the entire nation was treated to the best and worst episode of *Cops* ever recorded, as police accompanied O.J. Simpson's white Ford Bronco down the San Diego Freeway. Simpson, of course, was a suspect at the time in the murders of his ex-wife, Nicole, and her friend, Ron Goldman. So he did what any innocent person might do in his situation: he called a friend (former teammate Al Cowlings) and asked him to drive him away from the madness. The lunacy was compounded by people along his painstakingly documented route waving "Go, O.J., Go!" signs from overpasses.

Love Tap

June 19, 2000
Jeremy Mayfield vs. Dale Earnhardt

On the last lap of the Pocono 500, Jeremy Mayfield caught Dale Earnhardt in the final turn and gave the No. 3 car a little kiss that sent it high on the track. That token touch allowed Mayfield to blow by The Intimidator to take the checkered flag and receive a standing ovation. It also won Mayfield the admiration of his peers, who apparently didn't like to be Intimidated.

Payoff Pitch

June 20, 1982
Tom Watson

Tied for the U.S. Open lead with Jack Nicklaus, who had already completed his final round, Tom Watson overcooked a 2-iron off the tee of Pebble Beach's 209-yard par-3 17th into an impossible spot: in the intermediate rough back of the green, well above the hole, with 20 feet of lightning fast, sharply sloping green between ball and cup. Watching on a TV monitor, Nicklaus said there was "no way in the world" Watson could get his next shot close. Nicklaus was correct; Watson didn't get it close. He got it in. Taking advantage of a lucky break that found his ball sitting atop the rough instead of nestling down in it, Watson holed the short pitch. The birdie on 17 gave Watson a one-stroke lead, which he padded with another birdie on 18 to win his only U.S. Open title. It was the fourth time that Tom Terrific had edged the Golden Bear down the wire to win a major title. "I've had this happen to me before," Nicklaus said, "and I thought it would never happen again. And it did."

A Shot in the Heart

June 20, 1993
John Paxson

Phoenix was a city possessed by the Suns' run for an NBA title behind Charles Barkley, Dan Majerle, Kevin Johnson, and Danny Ainge. The Bulls were a team that never gave a thought to breaking a city's heart, and showed it by defeating Phoenix for their third straight title—and doing it on the road. The Bulls won the first two games in Phoenix, and Chicago fans started talking sweep. The Suns shut them up by taking two of three in Chicago. Back in Phoenix, with 3.9 seconds left in Game 6 and the Bulls trailing 98-96, Horace Grant found himself triple-teamed under his own basket. He kicked the ball out to the perimeter, where John Paxson calmly tossed in a three-pointer. The Suns had one last gasp, when Johnson flipped a soft floater toward the rim with about a second on the clock, but Grant swatted it away to secure the trophy. Paxson's shot, Suns coach Paul Westphal said later, "seemed like it was in the air for an hour. Every kid dreams of that in his backyard, and Paxson got to live out his dream."

The Hand of God

June 22, 1986
Diego Maradona

Argentina's Diego Maradona scored both goals in a
2-1 World Cup quarterfinal win over England. The
skill he displayed on the winning goal was admired by
all present, even the opposition. But that first goal?
Television replays showed that Maradona had deflected
the ball past the English goalkeeper with his hand. The
English team vehemently disputed the referee's non-
call, but the goal stood and virtually overnight went
into World Cup lore as the "Hand of God" goal. "I was
unhappy with the first goal because I thought he handed
it," said England coach Bobby Robson. "I didn't like the
second either, but I admired it."

The Act of a Statesman

June 24, 1995
Nelson Mandela

The president of South Africa, Nelson Mandela, had spent enough of his life in jail to warrant his holding a giant grudge toward anything and everything that represented white South Africa. Take, for instance, the national (but historically all-white) rugby team, who were facing off against New Zealand's feared All Blacks in the Rugby World Cup final. But rather than ignore the event, Mandela showed up for the game in Johannesburg wearing the famous No. 6 jersey of Springboks captain François Pienaar. South Africa won, 15-12. The honor of the moment "will always be a part of me," said Pienaar afterward. "After the win, President Mandela said thank you for what we have done for South Africa. I said we could never have done as much as he has."

$241,758 per Second

June 27, 1988
Mike Tyson vs. Michael Spinks

Michael Spinks was a cagey veteran who many experts thought would finally give Mike Tyson a real fight. Perhaps he could have, if Tyson had given him time. The heavyweight champ charged across the ring at the opening bell, and 91 seconds later Spinks was kissing the canvas hello and his career goodbye. Tyson made $22 million and didn't even break a sweat. At $13 million, Spinks had to settle for only $142,857 per second.

A Hawk Soars

June 27, 1999
Tony Hawk

At a time when the X Games were just beginning to go large, Tony Hawk pulled off the first 900—two-and-a-half rotations while skying above the halfpipe—in skateboarding competition. "This is the best day of my life," a still-jacked Hawk exulted over the cheers afterward. "I couldn't have done it without you fans." Even more was to come.

Bite of the Century

June 28, 1997
Mike Tyson vs. Evander Holyfield's Ear

With less than a minute left in the third round of his heavyweight title fight with Evander Holyfield, Mike Tyson took matters into his own mouth. In one of the strangest, most grotesque moments in sports history, Tyson bit off a chunk of Holyfield's ear and spit it out.

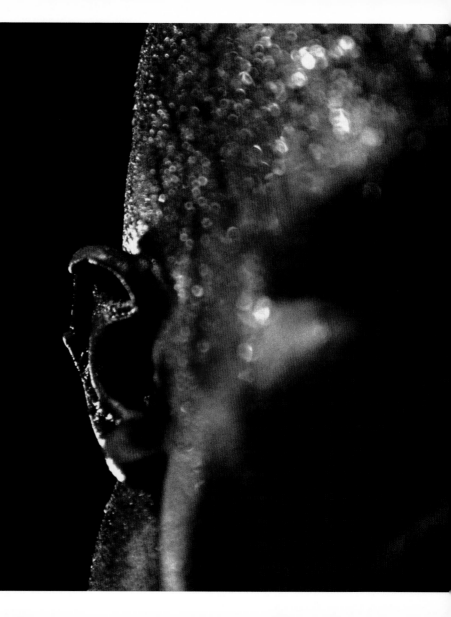

One-Man Show

June 29, 1994
Saeed Owairan

The Saudi team owed their stunning 1-0
upset of Belgium in the first round of
the World Cup to an incredible run by
No. 10 Saeed Owairan, who took control
of the ball near his own penalty box and
moved it by himself the entire length
of the field, leaving five Belgian players
in his wake before firing it home past
Michel Preud'homme, the best goalie in
the world at the time.

Disadvantage, Mr. Sampras

June 29, 2001
Pete Sampras

Third-round victories at Wimbledon for Pete
Sampras were usually ho-hum affairs, but
as he charged the net after serving to Sargis
Sargsian, he lost his footing a few paces from
the baseline. Next thing he knew, Sargsian's
return had bounced up the left leg of his
shorts and lodged there. After laughing on
the ground for a moment, Sampras called the
ball boy over with a crooked-finger "come
here" motion. Sampras was just having
some fun, even if the kid didn't think so
while vigorously shaking his head "no." Said
Sampras afterward: "I said it was all his.
He can pick up the ball if he wants it." He
declined. Can't say we blame him.

A Boy Among Men

June 30, 1998
Michael Owen

Upper lips were never stiffer than when England was reduced to playing with only 10 men on the field against Argentina in the World Cup's Round of 16. Fortunately for the Brits, one of the 10 was 18-year-old Michael Owen. With the score tied, 1-1, in the 16th minute, the teenager tore through the Argentine defense, took a pass near midfield, raced ahead, feinted left, cut to his right around an Argentine defender, and then scorched the ball back to his left and into the net for a 2-1 lead. England eventually lost in a penalty-kick shoot out after regulation time and two 15-minute overtimes left the score tied at 2-2. But "The Boy's Own" goal, so dubbed by the British press, made Owen an international star.

The Feeling Was Mutual

June 30, 2002
Bhutan vs. Montserrat

The game was conceived by two guys at a Dutch advertising agency who thought, Let's get the two lowest-ranked teams in the world to play a soccer game on the same day as the World Cup final. Sounds great, right? So the national team from the Caribbean nation Montserrat (ranked No. 203 in the world) flew around the globe to Thimphu, Bhutan, to play the Bhutanese national team. Bhutan (No. 202), the tiny Himalayan kingdom crunched between China and India, won 4-0 in front of 25,000 chanting fans at Thimphu's Changlimithang Stadium. At the finish, each of the team captains hoisted half of a silver trophy into the air, and a Montserrat player ripped off his jersey to reveal a handwritten message on his T-shirt: *We Love Bhutan.*

July

Pride of Cameroon

July 1, 1990
Roger Milla

England won the World Cup quarterfinals match 3-2 on an overtime penalty kick, but the Cameroon team, especially 38-year-old Roger Milla, who entered the game to start the second half with his team trailing 1-0, won the hearts of everybody who saw it. That Cameroon had made it to the knockout phase of the tournament was a shock enough to most soccer fans, but after knotting the game 1-1 on this penalty kick, Cameroon had more shock in store. Just five minutes later, Milla played a beautiful, soft ground ball to Eugene Ekeke, who dribbled past one defender and buried the ball in the net to put his team ahead—if ever so briefly— of one of the world's great powers in the game's biggest event.

Captain Courageous

July 1, 2004
Derek Jeter

Derek Jeter preserved the Yankees' 12th-inning tie with Boston by doing what he routinely does: whatever's necessary to win. Shading Trot Nixon up the middle with the lead run on third and two outs, Jeter had to sprint, stretch, and then dive directly into the stands to snare Nixon's foul halfway down the line in left. He emerged bruised and bloodied and had to leave the game. Who else would have sacrificed his body in that way? "A utility player trying to stay in the league," answered Yank Gary Sheffield. The Red Sox did take the lead in the 13th, but the Yankees, unwilling to lose a game their captain had already saved, pushed across two runs in the bottom of the inning for a 5-4 win.

Changing of the Guard

July 2, 1988
Steffi Graf vs. Martina Navratilova

What better place than Centre Court at Wimbledon to pass the torch of the most dominant player in the women's game? Steffi Graf, 19, cemented her hold on the No. 1 ranking by overpowering Martina Navratilova, 31, in the final two sets, 5-7, 6-2, 6-1, avenging straight-set losses to Navratilova at Wimbledon and the U.S. Open the year before. The victory was the third leg of Graf's trip to the first Grand Slam in women's tennis since Margaret Court did it in 1970. Beaten but predictably unbowed, Navratilova had this to say about her heir: "Steffi was hitting winners all over the place. She gets to balls no one else can. I got blown out the last two sets." Hail to the new queen!

Timmm-ber!

July 3, 1999
Jim Thome

If it weren't for Mark McGwire, Jim Thome would be a unanimous pick for baseball's Paul Bunyan. Can't you just see a row of checked lumberjack shirts, size XXL, in his closet? Exploding from an already open stance, Thome finished every swing (hit or miss) with his 6'4", 245-pound frame twisted around, parallel to the centerfield fence.
On this mighty cut, Thome made Jacobs Field look like a Little League park. The home run, easily the longest in the history of Cleveland's ballpark, was estimated at 511 feet and touched off an eight-run second inning for the Indians, who coasted to a 9-5 win over the Royals.

Not Björn Again

July 4, 1981
John McEnroe vs. Björn Borg

For five years, Björn Borg had ruled Wimbledon with an iron headband, winning 41 consecutive matches. But by the angry gestures of Mac's thumb, something wicked his way did come. Wicked, that is, in the aggressive play of 22-year-old John McEnroe. The finals battle had been building for a while—in their previous eight matches, the two had settled 12 of 27 sets by tiebreaker. On this day, McEnroe dropped the first set 4-6, then relentlessly pounded the Swede into the grass 7-6, 7-6, 6-4. The two tiebreakers were no contest, with McEnroe prevailing 7-1 and 7-4. "This is a triumph of McEnroe over Borg," the ornery new champion said. "Any time I can beat him, it's fine with me." And he said it with a smile.

Let's All Drink to That

July 4, 1984
Richard Petty

At age 47, Richard Petty posted his 200th and final career victory by winning the Firecracker 400 at Daytona. As 80,000 looked on from the stands, Petty won an easy victory over Cale Yarborough. President Ronald Reagan signaled the start of the Independence Day race using a radio aboard Air Force One—which is the machine the rest of the field would have needed to beat the man they called The King.

How Swede It Is

July 5, 1980
Björn Borg vs. John McEnroe

Björn Borg won the Wimbledon singles title with a thrilling five-set victory over John McEnroe, 1-6, 7-5, 6-3, 6-7, 8-6. The highlight was a marathon 34-point tiebreaker in the fourth set that McEnroe won to even the match. But Borg came back in the nearly-as-dramatic final set to win his 35th consecutive singles match and his fifth consecutive singles title at Wimbledon.

Making a Splash

July 6, 2002
Daryle Ward

Astros slugger Daryle Ward sent Pirates pitcher Kip Wells to the showers with a fifth-inning grand slam, the first home run at PNC Park in Pittsburgh to reach the Allegheny River on the fly. It takes a prodigious shot—at least 443 feet. And therein lies a bit of a mystery. Way out west, "splash hits" at the Giants' AT&T Park acquire instant cachet, even though it's much easier to hit San Francisco Bay than it is to reach the Allegheny. Certainly the Pirates lack a signature slugger like Barry Bonds, who can turn a splash into a *splash!* (Through the 2005 season, Bonds hit almost 63% of the balls that found the Bay.) Maybe the problem is that Pittsburgh isn't as picturesque as San Francisco. Or maybe the Pirates just need a nickname to rival McCovey Cove. May we suggest Clemente Creek?

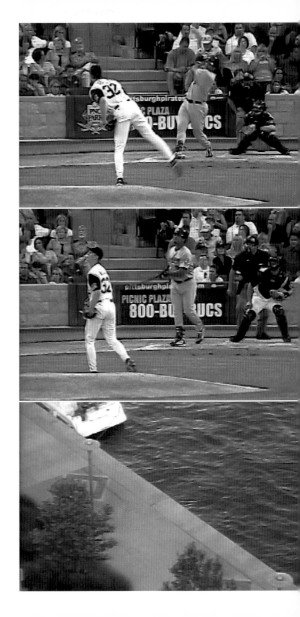

Queen of the Grass

July 7, 1990
Martina Navratilova vs. Zina Garrison

After holding her composure long enough to shake hands with Zina Garrison, Martina Navratilova fell to her 33-year-old knees to quietly soak in her ninth Wimbledon singles triumph. No one had won more, and it boosted her career mark at Wimbledon to 99-9. "I can't even comprehend winning *one* Wimbledon," said Garrison. "It's amazing that someone can do this nine times. She really believes this is her court and that no one can take it away from her." And for a good long time, nobody could.

This One's For You, Dad

July 7, 2001
Dale Earnhardt Jr.

In the first race at Daytona Speedway since his father was killed in a crash during the Daytona 500 five months earlier (*see* February 18, 2001), Dale Earnhardt Jr. won the Pepsi 400. After the third caution flag of the night was lifted, Junior was sixth with only six laps left. He moved up quickly, and with four laps to go he resumed the lead he'd held most of the race. Garagemate Michael Waltrip had his back. "I stayed and fought the battle for him," Waltrip said after the race. "At the end, I just pushed him home."

Valentin's Day

July 8, 1994
John Valentin

The story of the day was supposed to be the major-league debut of Seattle's 18-year-old shortstop, Alex Rodriguez. Evidently, Red Sox shortstop John Valentin didn't get the memo. In the top of the sixth, with nobody out and Mariners on first and second, a hit-and-run play went sour when Valentin caught a soft liner up the middle off the bat of Marc Newfield. He touched second to double up Mike Blowers and then tagged Keith Mitchell, who was chugging from first to second, to complete the 10th unassisted triple play in major-league history. And then, leading off the bottom of the sixth, Valentin hit the first of three Red Sox homers in the frame. The Red Sox won, 4-3. And that skinny teenager who would someday be known by all as A-Rod? 0-for-3.

Venus Ascendant

July 8, 2000
Venus Williams vs. Lindsay Davenport

Richard Williams' outlandish dreams for his daughters, nurtured first on the courts of Compton, Calif., came true on this day. His older daughter Venus joined Althea Gibson as the only African-American women to win Wimbledon. Even better, Venus—who'd watched younger sister Serena win the 1999 U.S. Open (*see* September 11, 1999)—became half of the first sister duo to win Grand Slam titles. Venus, 20, dismantled Lindsay Davenport's power game, 6-3, 7-6, with a combination of unrelenting force, speed, and a wingspan that consistently frustrated her opponent. Davenport was gracious in defeat: "You couldn't help but feel sorry for her last fall when Serena won first at the U.S. Open ... It's nice to see the monkey get off her back. Both Serena and Venus are going to win more Grand Slams." No kidding! The sisters would win eight of the next 12 Grand Slam singles titles: five for Serena and three for Venus.

Once More, Over the Wall

July 9, 2005
Danny Way

Ever dream about jumping over the Great Wall of China on a skateboard? No? Well, Danny Way did, and he went out and made his dream come true. You know Danny Way. He's that guy who jumped out of a helicopter and into a halfpipe a few times after being paralyzed from the waist up as a result of a surfing accident. Right, *that* Danny Way. After some time off from daredevilry to recover from seven surgeries, Way devised the MegaRamp, a 65-foot-high structure that launched him—at about 50 mph—over the more-than-2,000-year-old wall. After performing the stunt, what could Way possibly do for an encore? Easy. On each of his next three jumps, he added a 360° spin.

Out of His *Tête*

July 9, 2006
Zinedine Zidane vs. Marco Materazzi

Words were exchanged. In the 110th minute of the World Cup Final, Italy's Marco Materazzi said something to French star Zinedine Zidane as they walked toward midfield. Zizou took a few more steps past him, then turned around and planted his head directly and firmly on Materazzi's chest. Lip readers around the world have strained to see what Materazzi said that prompted the attack. Whatever, out came the red card and out went Zidane. The Zizou-less game stayed tied 1-1 as extra time ended. Italy then won the Cup on penalty kicks. Meanwhile, all of France was left to wonder, "*Mais pourquoi? Mais pourquoi?*"

Bra-Vo!

July 10, 1999
Brandi Chastain

Um, hello? Ms. Chastain? Did you know that you're on international television? Sure she did. The deal in soccer is that when you score the winning goal in a World Cup final, you're expected to rip your shirt off and go crazy. Fine. Let's just be careful about extending this tradition to other sports. It's all well and good if you have six-pack abs, flowing blond hair, and a prime-time smile. But we draw a serious line if John Daly ever wins another major.

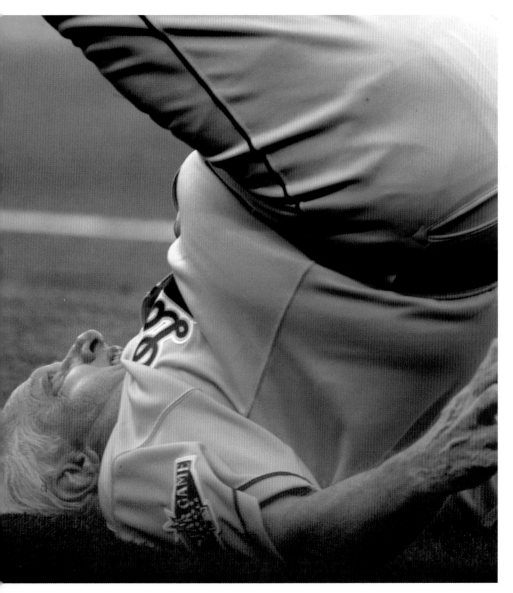

Humpty Dumpty Has a Great Fall

July 10, 2001
Tommy Lasorda

The most beloved raconteur in the game
acquires another story for his repertoire:
how he survived to talk another day
when the fat part of Vladimir Guerrero's
shattered bat hit his leg and sent him heels
over head from the third base coaching box.
"That was no big deal," said the 73-year-
old Lasorda. "I've taken tougher punches
than that in my time." Thanks, Tommy.
Meanwhile, in other All-Star Game news,
Cal Ripken Jr. and Tony Gwynn made their
farewell appearances.

Low Blow to Bowe

July 11, 1996
Riddick Bowe vs. Andrew Golota

Handlers became combatants. Spectators became participants. As a heavyweight bout ended at Madison Square Garden with the disqualification of Andrew Golota for repeated low blows to his opponent, Brooklyn's own Riddick Bowe, a melee was touched off by events in the ring. An incensed Bowe associate rushed Golota, who threw a swing; another Bowe associate smacked the Polish heavyweight across the head with a walkie-talkie, opening a cut and sending the fighter staggering through the restive crowd to the dressing room. Lou Duva, Golota's 74-year-old trainer, was knocked to the canvas and taken to the hospital on a stretcher. Skirmishes broke out in various areas of the arena, and ringside chairs were lofted into the ring. Miraculously, there were no major injuries—except to the pride and reputation of the Garden and the sport of boxing itself.

Vive le Zizou!

July 12, 1998
Zinedine Zidane

France isn't supposed to beat Brazil in a World Cup final, even if the match is played in a Parisian suburb before 80,000 soccer-mad Frenchmen screaming *Zizou! Zizou! Zizou!* But that's precisely what France did when Zizou—the extraordinary Zinedine Zidane—dominated play in the middle of the field, became the first player in 20 years to score two goals in a Cup final, and led his country to an astonishing 3-0 upset victory. That night, a million-plus jammed the Champs-Elysees to dance, sing, and cheer until dawn. Those French really know how to party.

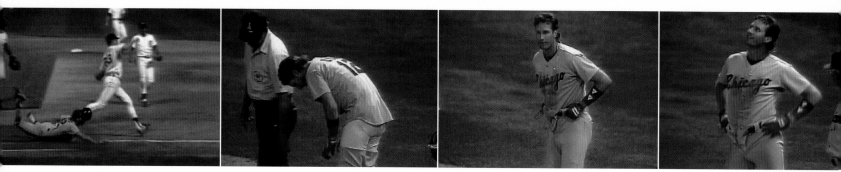

Take It Off!
Take It *All* Off!

July 16, 1990
Steve Lyons

Always one of the most intense players in baseball, White Sox utility player Steve Lyons slid hard into first to secure a fifth-inning single against Detroit. Not surprisingly, he ended up with his trousers full of dirt. (Pretty uncomfortable, we imagine.) Lyons promptly jumped up and dropped his pants to shake out the dirt. (Can you blame him?) It only dawned on him that thousands of people were enjoying his striptease when he heard the crowd laughing.

No Gooooooal!

July 17, 1994
Italy vs. Brazil

One hundred twenty minutes of play had produced not a single goal at the Rose Bowl, and for the first time the World Cup would be decided on penalty kicks. One by one, the best Brazilian and Italian players went head-to-head against the opposing goalies. After four rounds, Brazil was ahead 3-2, and Italy's last hopes rested on the foot of Roberto Baggio, the Azzurri's best player. As Baggio made his move to the ball, Brazilian goalie Claudio Taffarel dove the wrong way, and the coast was clear. But Baggio's rocket to the unguarded half of the net sailed just over the top of the crossbar. No goal, and the Brazilians raised their fourth World Cup trophy.

And the Oscar Goes to ...

July 17, 2001
Lance Armstrong

Up ahead was the steep 8.6-mile climb through 21 hairpin turns to the mountain resort of L'Alpe d'Huez, the final big climb in the Alps. At the back of the pack was Lance Armstrong, looking like a guy in need of an ambulance—huffing, puffing, seemingly on the verge of throwing up. Then, all of a sudden, he came to life. Passing archrival Jan Ullrich of Germany, Armstrong shot him a quick look that said, "Suckah!" The heavy breathing had been an act. "A bluff," Armstrong said later of his behavior. "Sometimes you have to play that game a little bit." Armstrong pulled away from the pack to win his first stage and set up his third straight Tour de France victory.

Frenchman's Folly

July 18, 1999
Jean Van de Velde

Since people first began knocking little balls around sheep meadows, acts of self-destruction have been commonplace (think: Phil Mickelson at the 2006 U.S. Open). But Jean Van de Velde's meltdown in the British Open at Carnoustie was in excruciatingly painful slow motion. The Frenchman managed to surrender a three-stroke lead in just one hole—the 72nd. After a wild drive right, Van de Velde's 2-iron shot crashed into the grandstand and kicked into deep rough (think: *Tin Cup*). A weak third shot left him in the water in front of the green. The sight of the forlorn Van de Velde with his trousers hiked up deciding to take a drop and a penalty stroke rather than attempt to hit his submerged ball out of Barry Burn represented the first sound judgment call he'd made to that point on the most important golf hole he'd ever played. A triple-bogey 7 let Van de Velde prolong his agony in a three-man, four-hole playoff. He finished in a tie for second with Justin Leonard. Scotland's Paul Lawrie was the 1999 British Open champion.

The Grinder

July 19, 1992
Nick Faldo

After losing a four-stroke lead down the stretch at the British Open at Muirfield, Nick Faldo looked more like the El Foldo of his younger days than the 35-year-old, four-time major winner who'd painstakingly built a reputation as the game's premier closer. "Sure, I thought I'd blown it," said Faldo. "But I turned it around. I went from the brink of disaster to the absolute ultimate." While Faldo was wobbling on the back nine, John Cook birdied 14, 15, and 16 to take a two-stroke lead, and Cook had an eagle putt on 17. Cook burned the edge with his eagle try, leaving two feet coming back. Just as he addressed the short putt, however, a roar went up: Faldo had birdied the 15th. Unhinged, Cook missed his birdie try, then went on to hit his 2-iron approach to 18 too far right. With a two-putt birdie at 17 and solid par at 18, Faldo claimed his third British Open title.

Ali Lights the Flame

July 19, 1996
Muhammad Ali

Who would be the last in the procession of stars, dignitaries, and local heroes who had carried the Olympic torch for 84 days and over 15,000 miles across America? Who would light the flame at the opening ceremony of the Olympic Games in Atlanta? Unlike most secrets, this one had been more closely guarded than the recipe for Atlanta's hometown beverage of choice, Coca-Cola. Then, when a shaking hand emerged from the shadows to take the torch from swimmer Janet Evans, we all felt foolish for not having guessed the answer. Who else *could* it have been but Muhammad Ali? Before Ali left the stadium, President Bill Clinton, who had officially opened the Games, put his hands on the shoulders of The Greatest and evoked the emotions behind the roar of the crowd: "They didn't tell me who would light the flame, but when I saw it was you, I cried."

Tour LeMond

July 23, 1989
Greg LeMond

Make up a 50-second deficit on Laurent Fignon in the last
15 miles of the 2,000-mile Tour de France? *Impossible!* as
the French would say. Then an American, Greg LeMond,
did it. Capping an improbable comeback from a hunting
accident that left 30 shotgun pellets in his body, LeMond
charged the final-stage time trial from Versailles to the
Champs-Elysees as no one ever had. Maintaining an
aerodynamic tuck while Fignon's unhelmeted ponytail
flapped in the breeze, LeMond shattered the previous Tour
time-trial record as he averaged 34 mph over the mostly
flat course. Had Fignon and LeMond left the starting line
together, LeMond's 58-second victory would have left
Fignon more than a half-mile behind. It all added up to
an eight-second win for LeMond that remains the closest
finish in Tour history.

Strugging It Off

July 23, 1996
Kerri Strug

With only the vault remaining, the USA women's gymnastics team seemed certain to win its first team gold. Only a train wreck could prevent the win. But when the penultimate vaulter, Dominique Moceanu, came up short twice—landing ingloriously on her backside—it was left to Kerri Strug to cinch the deal. But on her first run, Strug also ended up on her backside. Worse still, she came up gimpy. As it would turn out, Strug's score—butt-landing and all—was good enough to win the gold. But no one knew that at the time. So back she went, and quicker than you can say "America's Sweetheart," she flew toward the vault, flipped, and landed. She'd nailed it! Nailed it *and* her ankle. Strug bunny-hopped on one foot to turn toward the judges, then collapsed in pain. But she had nailed it, and the gold.

The Pine Tar Incident

July 24, 1983
George Brett

It was a toss-up who would choke first—
George Brett, from the massive wad of
chew in his mouth, or the umpires at
the hands of Brett, who had good reason
to go postal. He'd just hit a two-run
dinger off of Goose Gossage to put his
team ahead of those damned Yankees.
But Yanks skipper Billy Martin figured
if you can't beat 'em, throw the rule
book at 'em, so he had the home plate
ump measure the amount of pine tar on
Brett's bat. The rule said tar couldn't
extend more than 18 inches above the
handle. The ump measured the tar, found
Brett in violation of the rule, and recalled
the home run. It's never been officially
reported exactly what Brett said as he
charged the umps, and it won't be here.
Suffice it to say that Brett disagreed with
the call. The league eventually overturned
the disallowed homer, and the Royals
won the game when it was resumed a
month later. Martin held the reversal in
such disdain that he started ace lefty Ron
Guidry in centerfield during the official
end of the game.

Going Up? Otis Elevates!

July 25, 1992
Otis Nixon

Andy Van Slyke must have thought his one-out drive off Alejandro Peña would give his Pirates a 2-1 ninth-inning lead, ending Atlanta's bid for a 13th straight win. What Van Slyke didn't count on was Otis Nixon, in full stride, planting his left cleat on the padding of the 10-foot centerfield fence and leaping up to intercept Van Slyke's line shot. Jaws dropped. "I used to watch Willie Mays make great catches," said Nixon after the game. "I don't know where that ranks." His outfield partner, David Justice, had no doubt: "That's the best play I ever saw."

Perfect Response

July 28, 1994
Kenny Rogers

Despite the fact that not a single Angel had reached first base against him, Rangers lefty Kenny Rogers said the thought of a perfect game never entered his mind until the start of the ninth inning. And wouldn't you know it, the instant he started to think about it, Rogers threw a pitch that the Angels' Rex Hudler lashed into right centerfield for an almost certain gapper. Even Rogers said later, "I never thought he was going to get it." The "he" was rookie centerfielder Rusty Greer, who left his feet to make a diving, backhanded catch to preserve the 12th perfect game in the modern era, and just the third by a southpaw.

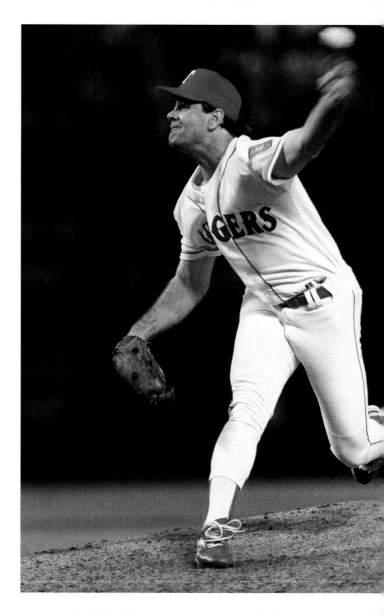

The Big Splash

July 29, 1992
Albin Killat

It's not as if he was the drunk uncle at a pool party. In fact, Germany's Albin Killat had, at times, shared the lead in the Olympic 3-meter springboard competition. But on his eighth dive, Killat took one in the gut. After leaping from the board for a forward 3 somersault, Killat landed—*splat!*—right on his stomach. A belly flop! In the Olympics! The British judge added to the ignominy by awarding Killat a score of 0, dropping the German to dead last.

Golden Oldie

July 29, 1996
Carl Lewis

At 35, Carl Lewis was more like 350 in long jump years, a pensioner who should have been in the broadcast booth or watching from the stands. Instead, on his third attempt in the Olympic long jump final, Lewis flew 27'10¾", his best jump at sea level since the Barcelona Olympics four years earlier. When he landed, he had his fourth consecutive gold in the same event—an honor shared only with discus thrower Al Oerter—and the ninth gold medal of his career.

August

Va-rooom!
Va-rooom!

August 1, 1996
Michael Johnson

One's an endurance test, the other's a drag race. That pretty much sums up why no Olympian in history had ever won the 400 meters and the 200 meters in the same Games. Until Michael Johnson. When Johnson won the 400 in Atlanta, he set an Olympic record of 43.49 seconds. Pretty remarkable. But what he then did in the 200 was positively mind-bending. Johnson left the field in his dust and set a world record of 19.32 seconds, three-tenths of a second faster than the previous best time ever, also run by Johnson. Three-tenths of a second may not sound like much, but in the 200 meters it's huge. His opponents were so amazed that Ato Boldon, the bronze medalist from Trinidad and Tobago, felt a mere handshake couldn't communicate his awe at what Johnson had done, so Boldon bowed respectfully to Johnson on the podium instead. Later he said, "I came off the turn and he went by. All I saw was a blue blur."

Old Timer's Day

August 2, 1992
Jackie Joyner-Kersee

By Olympic standards, Jackie Joyner-Kersee, at 30, was ancient when she won her second gold medal in the heptathlon, the seven-event track-and-field competition that is exhausting just to contemplate. No woman had ever won the heptathlon twice, and after her victory in the 800 meters, which clinched the gold, she took a victory lap waving a tiny American flag. During the lap, she ran into former decathlon gold medalist Bruce Jenner, who told her, "You're the greatest athlete in the world, man or woman." She certainly was that day.

Sticking a Perfect 10

August 3, 1984
Mary Lou Retton

With just one vault left in the Olympic women's gymnastics competition, 16-year-old pixie Mary Lou Retton needed a perfect 10 to win the gold in the women's all-around. A 9.95 would tie Retton for the top spot. No American woman had ever won a gold in the all-around in Olympic history, so the pressure was high. "I vault best under pressure," Retton said, sporting the big smile that helped make her the original America's Sweetheart. "It makes me fight harder. I knew if I stuck that vault, I'd win it. I kept thinking, *Stick! Stick! Stick!* I knew I had to get a 10." She did just that, with a full back somersault in the layout position, spiced with a twist. "I had goose bumps going up and down me," said Retton. "I knew from the takeoff, I knew from the run—I just knew it."

Lean on Me

August 3, 1992
Derek Redmond

Jim Redmond, father of British 400-meter man Derek Redmond, was in the stands during the Barcelona Olympics watching his son run his signature event when Derek stopped, rendered immobile by a pulled hamstring. The runner had battled injuries his entire career and had dropped out of the Olympics in 1988 with an Achilles tendon injury. This time, though, Redmond was going to finish the race no matter what. He struggled to his feet and took a few painful steps. Then, deciding to "Just Do It" like the slogan on his hat said, the elder Redmond appeared on the track and helped his son finish, steadying him for every excruciating step. "You don't have to do this," Jim said to his son. "You don't have to put yourself through this." When Derek insisted that he was going to finish, Jim replied, "Well, then, we're going to finish this together." And they did, while the capacity crowd roared its approval even as security guards and track officials tried to halt the pair. "I don't speak Spanish," said Jim, "and I wasn't going to be stopped by anything."

If at First You Don't Succeed ...

August 4, 1989
Dave Stieb

Twice in the previous season, Toronto's Dave Stieb had lost a no-hitter when he had just a single batter to get out. Now, with two down in the ninth, Roberto Kelly of the Yankees lined a double to left, this time robbing Stieb of a perfect game. "If I haven't gotten a no-hitter after three times," Stieb said after the game, "I doubt if I ever will." C'mon, Dave, what kind of attitude is that? (P.S.: Stieb did get his no-hitter the following season, the first in Blue Jays history.)

Respect Your Elders—or Else

August 4, 1993
Nolan Ryan vs. Robin Ventura

It was right out of *The Three Stooges*. Legendary
flamethrower Nolan Ryan, 46, sent a little chin
music Robin Ventura's way, and Ventura, 26,
charged the mound to teach the old geezer a
lesson. But wait! Ryan, who threw his first pitch
in the big leagues the year before Ventura was
born, got the White Sox punk in a headlock and
started whomping on top of his head. The Rangers'
quatrogenarian landed six knocks to Ventura's
noggin before a cluster of other players swarmed
the two. Now if only Ryan had brought out a pair of
pliers and clamped them on Ventura's nose ...

High and Mighty

August 5, 1991
Sergei Bubka

He held 13 outdoor and 15 indoor world records and won the
World Championships in 1983 and 1987, along with Olympic
gold in 1988. There wasn't much Russian pole vaulter Sergei
Bubka hadn't done with a long pole, really, except clear 20 feet
outdoors—something no one had ever done. So at the Dag Galan
Grand Prix meet in Malmö, Sweden, Bubka capped a remarkable
career by doing just that: 20 feet, ¼ inch.

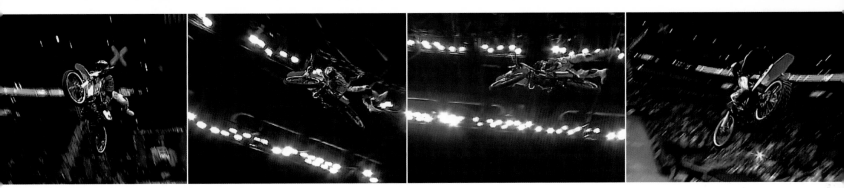

Hero Roll

August 5, 2004
Chuck Carothers

The move was officially known as a seat-grab 360 body varial, but Chuck Carothers referred to it as the Carolla—a combination of "Carothers" and "roll." And, brother, did Chuck ever roll! He became the first moto X rider to stick the move in competition. Carothers rocketed 40 feet into the air, let go of the handlebars, pushed off his seat, and with his body parallel to the ground, executed a barrel roll before grabbing the bars and pulling himself back onto his bike to land. "I'm pretty sure I had some luck on my side," Carothers said. If by "pretty sure" he meant "out of my freakin' mind," we couldn't agree more.

Local Boy Makes Good

August 6, 1994
Jeff Gordon

Growing up, Jeff Gordon lived within 15 miles of the Indianapolis Motor Speedway. But when he spurned Indy racing for stock cars, he presumably gave up his chances of ever winning a big race at the Brickyard. Not so. When NASCAR scheduled its first race at the speedway, the Brickyard 400, it was the young Gordon who drove home a winner. "To me," said the 23-year-old Gordon, "this is the Indianapolis 500 of stock car racing." He led for most of the day, and moved out in front for good in lap 156 of 160.

Not All Hits Are Created Equal

August 7, 1999
Wade Boggs

Twenty-two men before him had recorded 3,000 or more major-league hits, but not a one had ever notched No. 3,000 with a dinger. So it was all the more remarkable that Tampa Bay's Wade Boggs, who made his living slapping singles and doubles, pounded his milestone hit into the seats at Tropicana Field. (Only 117 of his previous 2,999 hits had been homers.) After singles in the third and fourth innings brought him to the precipice, Boggs turned on an offering from Cleveland's Chris Haney. "I knew it was gone," Boggs said. "I thought, 'Oh, my God, it's a home run, and I'll never get that ball back.'" Not that he was really upset or anything: after circling the bases, Boggs celebrated by kissing home plate.

Long Hit, Long Catch

August 7, 2002
Terrence Long

With two out and two on in the bottom of the ninth and his team trailing 3-2, Manny Ramirez did what he was paid gazillions by the Red Sox to do: hit a big ball in a big moment. A's reliever Billy Koch had put the go-ahead runs, in the form of Trot Nixon and Johnny Damon, on base. Ramirez had homered in the fourth, and now his hero shot to deep right-center was heading out of the park. Except the hero was Oakland's Terrence Long, who lunged over Fenway's short wall to bring back what would have been the game-winner.

Let There Be Light

August 8, 1988
Wrigley Field

At 6:09 p.m. CT, a switch was hit in Wrigley Field, 540 floodlights flashed on, and the last team in the majors to play ball only in the daytime joined the modern era—or lost its soul, depending on your point of view. The baseball gods were evidently not too pleased. In the third inning of the game against the Phillies, a dust storm briefly brought play to a stop. Then there was thunder and lightning, and finally there was rain. "Next," said one Cubs fan, "there will be a plague of locusts." The game was finally called as the thunderstorm continued.

Be Careful What You Wish For

August 8, 1992
U.S. Olympic Basketball

Having grown weary of its college kids getting beaten, the United States sent perhaps the best basketball team ever assembled to the Olympic Games to let the world know once and for all who was king of the playground. The Dream Team, as the U.S. squad was quickly dubbed, was mighty indeed. Michael Jordan, Charles Barkley, Larry Bird, Magic Johnson, Patrick Ewing, Karl Malone, Scottie Pippen, David Robinson, Clyde Drexler, and John Stockton gave up their summer vacations to wear the red-white-and-blue. And yes, they won the gold, hammering Croatia 117-85. And yes, it was boring. And yes, it started what was pretty much the ruination of the fun in watching Olympic basketball. And yes, in case you haven't guessed by now, we're not fans of Dream Teams.

Trading Places

August 9, 1988
Wayne Gretzky

After winning four Stanley Cups and eight MVP titles and setting 43 league-scoring marks as an Edmonton Oiler, Wayne Gretzky asked to be traded to the dustbin of professional hockey, Los Angeles. The Oilers got a big package for him: three top draft picks, $10 million—and a townful of fans decked out in mourning clothes. That's what you get when your hometown hero marries a Playboy Playmate and goes Hollywood. The Mayor of Edmonton, Laurence Decore, put it best: "It's like taking all the bridges away and saying, 'Edmonton, this is what you're going to look like.'"

Nipped by a Budd

August 10, 1984
Zola Budd vs. Mary Decker

In a highly anticipated Olympic 3,000-meter showdown in Los Angeles, American Mary Decker was favored over the shoeless Zola Budd, a South African who had been granted British citizenship in order to skirt the ban on athletes from her apartheid-practicing homeland. Midway through the race, the two seemingly tangled legs and Decker went down—and out of the race. Budd ran on, and Decker, in a snapshot that summed up her career, lay defeated on the track.

Bunker Mentality

August 11, 1986
Bob Tway vs. Greg Norman

Greg Norman's tumultuous season, in which he led each of the four majors going into the final round, looked like it would end with him winning two of them. He had folded under Jack Nicklaus' charge at the Masters, wilted after being taunted by a fan at the U.S. Open, and won the British Open at Turnberry. Now, in the PGA Championship at the Inverness Club in Toledo, Ohio, Norman led Bob Tway by four shots with nine holes to play. But eight holes later there was the Great White Shark on the 18th tee in a tie with Tway. Still, Norman looked to be in the driver's seat. Tway had pushed his ball right into deep rough. From a dodgy lie, he ended up in a greenside bunker. Norman hit the green with a wedge, but excessive spin caused the ball to yank back just beyond the fringe. Even then, Norman appeared to have the upper hand, until Tway exploded from the bunker and holed the shot to win. "I wasn't trying to make the sand shot," Tway told the press afterward. "The odds against making a shot like that at 18, I don't even know. I may never make one of them again in my career." He didn't—not that that was any solace to Norman.

Collision Center

August 11, 2005
Mike Cameron and Carlos Beltran

The play began innocently enough, with San Diego pinch-hitter David Ross floating a fly ball toward shallow right center during a Mets-Padres day game. What happened next had its roots in the off-season, when Mike Cameron, the Mets' Gold Glove centerfielder, was moved to right to make room for Carlos Beltran. As Beltran moved toward the gap and the ball, Cameron did the same from the other direction. A typical rightfielder might have given way, but Cameron, a centerfielder at heart, lived to hunt down the ball. The two dove for the ball at the same instant and hit head-on, dropping to the field and leaving the grass bloodied. "I don't remember anything of what happened," Beltran said. "I felt like I was kind of lost." The two ended up in separate hospitals. Cameron was put on the DL with a broken nose, multiple fractures of his cheekbones, and a concussion. Beltran had a sore left shoulder and a cut on his left cheek. The Mets' Marlon Anderson was one of the first to reach the two players. "I couldn't imagine being a paramedic going to the scene of a wreck," said Anderson, "because that's pretty much what this was, a wreck."

Minus 12 in Plus Fours

August 13, 1989
Payne Stewart

The man who almost made knickers fashionable again was resplendent this day at Kemper Lakes near Chicago. Resplendent not only in his blue and orange stripes—when did the Bears start playing golf?—but also on the course, where he shot a blistering 5-under 31 on the back nine on the final day of the PGA Championship. For Payne Stewart, claiming the victory with his 12-under 276 depended just as much on Mike Reid, who was leading by three strokes with only three holes to play. Reid's collapse—a bogey, a double-bogey, then a missed birdie putt on the final hole—dropped him to 277. "I feel sorry for Mike," Stewart said after taking his first major title. "But I'm not going to kid you about how I feel."

Eyes Wide Shut

August 15, 1999
Sergio Garcia

Nineteen-year-old Sergio Garcia of Spain had Tiger by the tail at the PGA Championship. Garcia was stalking Woods, trailing by just two shots, and had the crowd on his side. Chants of "*Ser-gee-o! Ser-gee-o!*" thundered across Medinah. But on the 16th hole, after his drive had settled between the roots of a tree 189 yards from the pin, Garcia was looking at an almost certain bogey. "I started to tell him to pitch out," said Garcia's caddie, Jerry Higginbotham. "But I've seen this kid pull off so many things, I figured I'd let him go ahead." Garcia took a mighty lash with his 6-iron, closing his eyes as the club neared impact, fully expecting the club to reverberate off the roots or the ball to ricochet off the tree. But the ball came out clean, curved beautifully from left to right, and rolled onto the green. As the shot took off, Garcia took off after it, running and performing a leaping scissor kick in an attempt to see where the ball ended up. Garcia made his par. Woods held on to win the tournament, but it was Garcia who won the hearts of the fans.

Double the Fun

August 16, 2002
Mike Metzger

In the 2002 X Games, Mike Metzger became the first moto X rider to land back-to-back backflips. How'd you feel on the first flip, Mike? "It felt like when I was on my bicycle. A lot bigger, though, and a lot more time in the air." How about that second one? "After I landed the first, I knew I had the second. I knew I was gonna pull it. I was planning on doing it in practice, but I figured I would wait 'til the finals." Over three days, Metzger won the freestyle and big air events and took second in Step Up, winning an estimated $100,000.

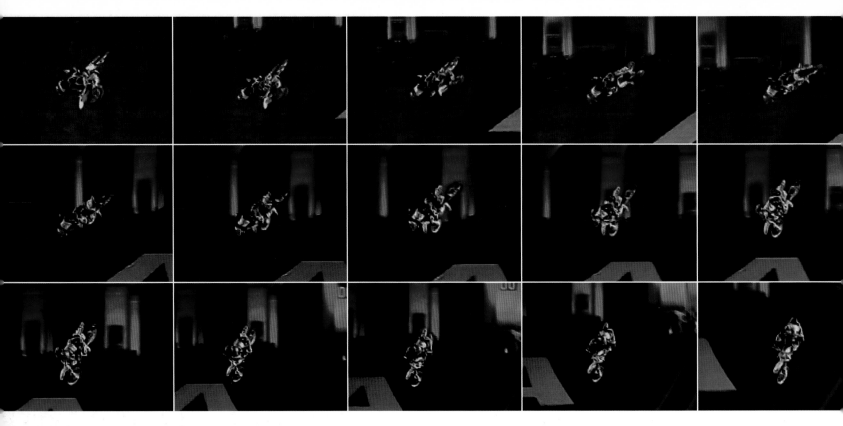

360 Reasons Why

August 16, 2003
Travis Pastrana

Start with a garden-variety moto X backflip. Throw in a complete horizontal rotation happening at the same time. Fall off your bike on your first attempt. Pull off the new trick, a 360° barrel-roll backflip, in bonus time at the X Games to win the Moto X Freestyle competition. Awesome!

Look, Ma— No Hands!

August 17, 2002
Mat Hoffman

At the scary old age of 30, Mat Hoffman came out of retirement to compete in the X Games. Just so everyone knew he was there, Hoffman landed the first—and so far, only—no-hands 900 in X Games history. "I've been dreaming about it for three weeks now," Hoffman said. "I've been walking around and, periodically, I go into a spin and my hands come off."

Little Big Man

August 18, 2001
Danny Almonte

Of all the Rolando Paulino All-Stars who brought
Little League World Series fame to the Bronx,
improbably tall pitcher Danny Almonte was the
most electrifying. In this tournament outing, he
hurled a perfect game, mixing heat that registered
up to 70 mph with wicked breaking balls. The game
drew national attention and capped off a big league-
caliber performance for Almonte, who mowed down
46 batters in three starts during the tournament. If
it looked at times like Almonte was a man playing
with boys, well, the metaphor fits the facts. A few
days after his perfect game, it was revealed that
Almonte was 14 years old, two years older than the
maximum age for the LLWS. The team was stripped
of its third-place finish in the tournament, and
coach Ronaldo Paulino was banned from all future
Little League activities.

One Phelps Sweep

August 19, 2004
Michael Phelps

With a gold in the 200-meter individual medley, Michael Phelps took another step closer to the legendary Olympian Mark Spitz. This was his third individual gold of the Athens Games. The next day he grabbed his fourth individual gold to tie a Spitz record. He didn't match Spitz's seven overall golds, but he did win eight total medals, the most ever for an American at one Olympiad.

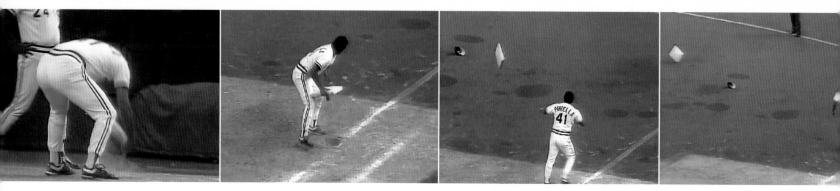

Base Behavior

August 21, 1990
Lou Piniella

The fans at Riverfront Stadium chanted, "Lou! Lou!" after Reds manager
Lou Piniella got tossed during an 8-1 win over the Cubbies. Why the
adulation? Sweet Lou was displeased with a call at first and with getting
ejected, so he took first base and threw it. Twice. "I just watched it in slow
motion, and it was impressive," said Reds first baseman Hal Morris after the
game. "On the replay, he threw it a lot farther than I thought he did. Some
guys think it should be a new Olympic event." The Base Put?

High Anxiety

August 24, 2004
Yelena Isinbayeva vs. Svetlana Feofanova

As the Athens night wore on, Russian pole vaulters Yelena Isinbayeva and Svetlana Feofanova were playing a game of centimeters. Feofanova held the lead at 4.75 meters. After two dramatic misses at 4.70 and 4.75 meters, Isinbayeva was in line for a disappointing third. "I don't want to boast, but I'm not used to bronzes and I'm not used to losing," Isinbayeva said later. "It's all or nothing with me." On her third and final vault, with much of the world watching, she went for the win. Setting the bar at an even 4.80, she sailed over with ease. Just to kick a little sand at Feofanova, Isinbayeva then cleared 4.85 and 4.91 meters to add a world record to her Olympic gold medal.

Beachhead Assault

August 24, 2004
Misty May and Kerri Walsh

To say that Americans Misty May and Kerri Walsh were the dominant pair in women's beach volleyball is like saying there's a lot of sand at the beach. At one point, starting in 2003, they won 90 straight matches and 15 consecutive titles, and their streak was interrupted only because May suffered an injury. At the Athens Olympics, the 6'3" Walsh and the 5'10" May didn't drop a set, and in the final against Brazil, they made it look easy, with Walsh hammering a spike just inside the line to cap a 21-17, 21-11, gold medal performance.

Not So Fast

August 27, 2004
Marion Jones to Lauryn Williams

By the time Marion Jones ran her leg of the 4 x 100-meter relay at the Athens Olympics, the woman who had once been the fastest in the world was medal-less in Greece. But with a solid sprint in the second leg of the relay, she could redeem herself. With 100-meter silver medalist Lauryn Williams waiting ahead of her, Jones appeared to relax her stride. Williams broke out quickly as Jones cried for her to slacken the pace. Each of Jones' sweeps of the baton toward her hand missed their target, and the U.S. team was left to watch the Jamaicans take gold. "It exceeded my wildest dreams," Jones said after the disappointing finish. "In a negative sense."

A Face in the Crowd

August 29, 2004
Vanderlei de Lima

Brazil's Vanderlei de Lima was the surprise front-runner at the 22-mile point of the marathon at the Athens Olympics. With a lead of 30 seconds, he was looking strong. We'll never know whether he could have held on to win, because suddenly a psychotic, defrocked priest named Cornelius Horan emerged from the crowd wearing a sign on his back that read: "The Grand Prix Priest Israel Fulfillment of Prophecy Says the Bible." Horan pushed de Lima from the center of the course into the crowd of spectators, forcing the runner to a complete stop. When he resumed running, de Lima still held the lead, but he was eventually passed by Stefano Baldini of Italy and Meb Keflezighi of the U.S. "I couldn't defend myself," de Lima later said. "I was totally concentrated on my race. It's extremely difficult to find that rhythm again."

Shooting Stars

August 30, 1997
Comets vs. Liberty

The freshly minted league had only eight teams, but the WNBA didn't lack for a superstar. Leading scorer Cynthia Cooper had carried her Houston Comets the whole maiden season, so her 25-point performance against the New York Liberty in the championship game came as no surprise. Nor did her pinpoint passing to set up Tina Thompson for several of her 18 points in the 65-51 victory. The championship core of Cooper, Thompson, and Sheryl Swoopes stuck together, and the Comets held onto the hardware through the 2000 season, after which Cooper retired (for the first time) and the Comets came back to Earth.

Sometimes You Just Get a Feeling

August 31, 1997
Jeff Gordon

Jeff Gordon had a feeling. A lot was on the line at Darlington Raceway. A $1 million bonus. A chance to make it three straight wins at the Southern 500, NASCAR's oldest race. Because of what it meant to the sport, it was one race every driver wanted to win—bad. Gordon sensed before the engines were started that things might get ugly down the stretch. "The desire will take over if I have a shot with two or three laps to go," predicted Gordon. "I might just have to get really aggressive if I have a chance." With his car struggling the better part of the day, Gordon made up huge chunks of track after clouds moved in and cooled the surface. As he exited Turn 4 and headed for the final lap, Gordon held the lead, but then Jeff Burton tried to pass him on the low side. Gordon moved to block Burton and got a few angry love taps for the maneuver. Gordon recovered quickly to force Burton hard to the inside apron as they approached Turn 1. Once again the two cars hit, this time a bit more aggressively, before Gordon pulled ahead for good. He won by .144 seconds, just inches ahead of Burton. Not surprising, really, seeing as he already knew what was going to happen.

September

Jimmy Blows Out the Candles

September 2, 1991
Jimmy Connors

In his fourth-round U.S. Open match against Aaron Krickstein—a player 15 years his junior—Jimmy Connors waged a birthday battle in New York that was vintage Connors. He began the day by turning 39, then ground his way into the fifth set taking the vocal fans along for the ride, fist-pumping and hustling all the way. "This was 20,000 people making the noise of 60,000," said Connors after prevailing 7-4 in a tiebreaker for the fifth set. "By the fifth set, he's under tension and I'm riding the tide, I'm flying. Was I ever gonna give up? Oh, no! Hell, no!" Connors fist-pumped and hustled his way into his 16th Open quarterfinal in 21 tries.

Beating the Odds

September 4, 1993
Jim Abbott

Yankee lefty Jim Abbott wanted people to forget he was born without a right hand, and he always figured the best way to do that was to make them remember he was a talented pitcher. In a game against the Indians at Yankee Stadium in the middle of a tight pennant race with the crowd of 27,225 fans on their feet and cheering every pitch, Abbott retired Kenny Lofton and Felix Fermín, then forced Carlos Baerga, one of the Indians' best hitters, to ground softly to short to sew up a no-hit shutout. "I didn't know how to act out there," said Abbott, who walked five but allowed no runner beyond first base. "I didn't know whether to be supremely confident or supremely thankful. I guess it's a little bit of both."

Gut Check

September 5, 1996
Pete Sampras

After losing the second point of a fifth-set tiebreaker in the quarterfinals of the U.S. Open, Pete Sampras paused for a moment to ... vomit. It wasn't so much the way he was playing against Alex Corretja—he won, after all: 7-6 (7-5), 5-7, 5-7, 6-4, 7-6 (9-7). Rather, it was simply the, uh, gut-wrenching ups and downs of the match.

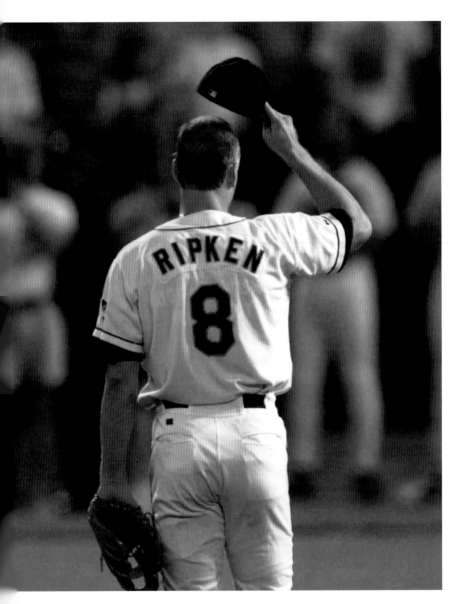

Just Another Day at the Office

September 6, 1995
Cal Ripken Jr.

The one major league baseball record that, not so long ago, everybody thought would last forever, fell. When a meeting between the Baltimore Orioles and the California Angels went into the record books as an official game, Cal Ripken Jr. had broken Lou Gehrig's mark of 2,130 consecutive games played. The icing on the cake for the 46,000-plus fans—including President Bill Clinton and Joe DiMaggio—jammed into Camden Yards was a Ripken homer into the leftfield seats in his second at-bat. (Oh, yeah, and Baltimore won 4-2.) So what did Ripken do after breaking the record? Take a couple of days off, play a little Sunday golf, head over to Maryland's Eastern Shore for the September bluefish run? Not exactly. He kept playing another six years, retiring after the 2001 season with his consecutive game streak up to 2,632. Now *that* record *will* last forever.

Homer Happy

September 7, 1993
Mark Whiten

Ever hear the name Mark Whiten? Only stone Rotisserie players of a certain age are likely to ID him as a switch-hitting outfielder with a little pop who played with nine different teams during an 11-year career that ended in 2000. He'll never be mentioned in the same breath with Ruth, Aaron, or Bonds. He won't have a plaque in Cooperstown. But for one magical night, Mark Whiten was one of the greatest hitters in baseball history. In the second game of a Cardinals-Reds doubleheader, Whiten—a Cardinal at the time—pounded out four homers and drove in a record-tying 12 runs. "I don't even have words to explain it, just amazement, I guess," Whiten said afterward. "Every time I hit it, I was, like, amazed."

Over and Out

September 8, 1998
Mark McGwire

Mark McGwire, his Popeye arms flexing their might yet again, as they had done already 61 times this summer, turned on the first pitch from Chicago Cubs righthander Steve Trachsel and pulled it hard, just barely making it over the wall as it hugged the leftfield foul pole. *No. 62!* As the ball cleared the wall, a jubilant McGwire missed first base as he leapt into the arms of Dave McKay, the Cardinals first base coach and McGwire's favorite batting practice pitcher. "That's the first time that I think I missed first base," McGwire told the press after the game. McKay had the presence of mind to usher McGwire back to tag the bag so the homer would be official.

Alabama Slammer

September 10, 2005
Tyrone Prothro

With Alabama trailing Southern Miss 21-10, Tyrone Prothro fired up his Crimson Tide teammates with a catch that was ... well, it was impossible. On fourth and 12, with a mad blitz in his face, Tide QB Brodie Croyle heaved a Hail Mary toward the goal line. Southern Miss DB Jasper Faulk had every inch of Prothro covered and his back to the ball, so Prothro reached around him, snagged the ball, and pinned it against Faulk's back as the two crashed onto the turf. Somehow, Prothro never lost control. After a review by the refs, the ball was placed on the 1 and Bama scored on the next play to spark a 30-21 victory. Following the game, his teammates started calling him ESPY—presciently, as it turned out. Prothro's impossible grab won the 2006 ESPY for Best Play.

Goodbye, Ty!

September 11, 1985
Pete Rose

Love him or hate him, think he belongs in Cooperstown or not, on one thing the whole baseball world agrees: Pete Rose could hit. On this night in Cincinnati, just 10 miles from where he played ball as a boy, Charlie Hustle, 44 and in his 23rd season in the majors, clipped a first-inning single off of San Diego's Eric Show for hit No. 4,192—one better than Ty Cobb, the guy he'd been chasing his entire career. "Thank you, Mr. President, for taking time from your busy schedule," said Rose to President Ronald Reagan during a postgame phone call. "You missed a good ball game." No kidding: the Reds shut out the Padres, 2-0.

Growing Up Fast

September 11, 1999
Serena Williams

She may have been Venus' little sister, but there was nothing little about Serena Williams' game at the U.S. Open. In her first Grand Slam final, 17-year-old Serena hammered Martina Hingis, the world's top-ranked player, 6-3, 7-6 (7-4). "Oh, my God, I won! Oh, my God," said Williams with both hands over her heart after Hingis played the game's final point out of bounds. "I thought, Should I scream, should I yell, or should I cry?" Williams said later. "And I guess I ended up doing them all."

Enough Is Enough

September 12, 1982
Dolphins vs. Jets

The idea that Don Shula's Miami Dolphins could fail to beat a team—*any* team—even once in eight consecutive games was almost unfathomable. But the Dolphins' record in their last eight meetings with the New York Jets was an ugly 0-7-1. So even though Miami led 24-14 midway through the third quarter, Shula wasn't about to ease off in game No. 9. With the ball on New York's 15, Dolphins QB David Woodley handed off to RB Tony Nathan for what appeared to be a prudent, by-the-book sweep that would reduce turnover risk and run time off the clock. Worst case scenario: settle for a field goal. And so, after sending Nathan on his way, Woodley did what savvy quarterbacks do, drifting away to stay out of harm's way. But then, Woodley took off down the field. Nathan pulled up, set his feet, and threw the ball across the field. Woodley, signal-caller turned wide receiver, grabbed the pass and waltzed into the end zone untouched. Final score: 45-28 (or 1-7-1 if you're looking at the big picture).

Playing Catch-Up

September 13, 1998
Sammy Sosa

After Mark McGwire hit No. 62 (*see* September 8, 1998), some of the steam went out of the riveting, season-long race between him and Chicago's Sammy Sosa. But only briefly. With two dingers against Milwaukee, Sosa caught up to McGwire at 62, also passing Roger Maris in the process. "Who'd have ever thought two people would do it in the same year?" said Sosa's teammate Mark Grace. "I hope Sammy gets the attention that he deserves." He did.

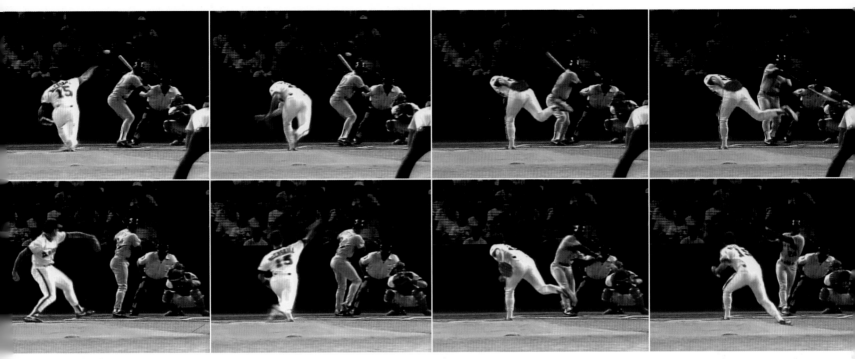

Like Father, Like Son

September 14, 1990
Ken Griffey Sr. and Ken Griffey Jr.

When Ken Griffey Sr. and Ken Griffey Jr. became teammates after the former's trade to the Mariners by the Reds, it set up a feat that will probably never be matched as long as baseball is played. In a game against the California Angels, the father drove a pitch into the seats in centerfield. As he touched the plate, the son was waiting to bat next. Junior stepped in, took three straight balls, got the green light—and launched one over the fence, just a little to the left of where the old man had. Sixteen years later, the Griffeys still hold the record for most back-to-back home runs by a father and son with the same first name: one. Says here that they always will.

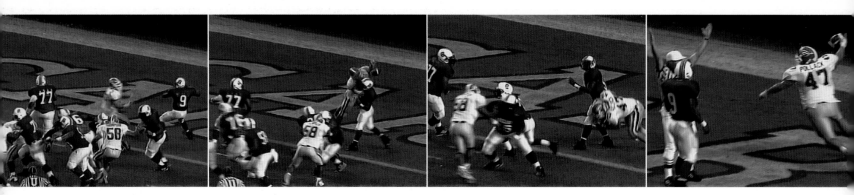

Hanna and Her Bulldogs

September 14, 2002
South Carolina vs. Georgia

The South Carolina-Georgia game was delayed for nearly an hour by Tropical Storm Hanna, and when action finally got under way in Columbia, it was still pouring rain. The more than 84,000 Gamecocks fans who stuck it out through the downpour gasped when Georgia's David Pollack turned a sack into this zero-yard interception and touchdown in the Cocks' end zone to make the score 10-0. But Lou Holtz's plucky Gamecocks mounted a final rally. Trailing 13-7 with 12 seconds remaining and poised on the Georgia 2, Holtz called QB Corey Jenks to toss back to tailback Andrew Pinnock. With no extra help around to block, Pollack forced Jenkins to make an early pitch that Pinnock couldn't handle. Fumble. End of game.

Triple Jeopardy

September 15, 1987
Team Canada vs. Team USSR

A hockey goalie's worst nightmare is the three-on-one breakaway. But this breakaway, heading toward the Russian goalie in the third period of a 5-5 tie between Team Canada and the Soviet Union in the Canada Cup final, was just plain ridiculous: Mario Lemieux, Wayne Gretzky, and Larry Murphy (who was just along for the ride). At least it was over quick. Gretzky put the puck on Lemieux's stick, who promptly put it in the net, and the winning goal was in the books. The goal was Lemieux's 11th of the tournament and second game-winner of the championship series.

A Battle for the Ages

September 16, 1981
Sugar Ray Leonard vs. Thomas Hearns

They could have billed the bout to unify the welterweight division Speed Power vs. Power Speed. On the other hand, Sugar Ray Leonard vs. Thomas "Hit Man" Hearns had a nice ring to it. The match came near the tail end of a golden era for boxing, and it turned out to warrant all the advance buzz it generated. Deep into the fight, Hit Man (32-0) was having his way with Leonard (30-1). Sugar Ray appeared to be flagging in the 13th when he suddenly flashed an overhand right to the head that changed the course of the fight. Hearns hit the deck three times in the 13th—albeit twice on pushes. The fight was stopped at 1:45 of the 14th, with Hearns still on his feet but defenseless. "This was my toughest fight," said Leonard afterward, trying to squint through a left eye that was swollen shut. "It surpasses all of my professional accomplishments."

Just Dropping In

September 17, 2002
Paul Lo Duca

The Los Angeles Dodgers and the San Francisco Giants were slugging it out to see which team would take a one-game lead in the wild-card race. The Giants led 5-4 and had men in scoring position with two outs in the seventh when San Francisco pinch-hitter Damon Minor lofted a popout that drifted toward the Dodgers' dugout. LA catcher Paul Lo Duca rushed to the scene and made a spectacular sliding catch that took him right into the dugout, where his elated teammates covered him in backslaps. Somebody else went back to fetch his mask.

The Oldest Rookie

September 18, 1999
Jim Morris

When 35-year-old rookie Jim Morris took the mound for Tampa Bay, 16 years after he'd been drafted by the Brewers, the biggest question was, Who'd play him in the movie? A year before, Morris was a physics teacher and baseball coach in Big Lake, Texas, population 2,885. Coach made a bet with his players that if they made the state playoffs, he'd try out for the big leagues. Thanks to a still-blazing 98-mph fastball, Morris soon joined the Durham Bulls, and from there moved up to the Devil Rays. His career may have been short, pitching in 21 games over two seasons, but Morris' story will undoubtedly be watched over and over on *The Rookie* DVD—starring Dennis Quaid.

That's Gotta Smart

September 19, 1988
Greg Louganis

It could hardly have been more embarrassing, if Greg Louganis had belly-flopped Instead, during the preliminary round of the 3-meter springboard at the Seoul Olympics, Louganis smashed his head into the board while trying to do a reverse somersault. The flub opened a gash that required five stitches, but he was able to return to competition the same day. "I didn't realize I was that close to the board," Louganis explained. "But I think my pride was hurt more than anything else." Only a day later, he won a gold medal in the event, then followed it with another gold in platform diving, thus becoming the first man ever to win gold medals in both events in consecutive Olympics.

Paddling Into History

September 19, 2000
Eric Moussambani

Eric Moussambani learned to swim just eight months before in a river near his home in Malabo, Equatorial Guinea. Yet here he was in Sydney, competing in the Olympics in the 100-meter freestyle, thanks to the wild card rule that allows each country to enter one athlete in each event even if he or she doesn't meet the qualifying standard. After false starts by the other wild card entrants from Niger and Tajikistan, Moussambani found himself alone in his heat. No matter. At the starter's signal, he flopped into the pool and began to, well, flail away. At first, the spectators thought it was a joke. Then they realized they were witnessing one of those rare Olympic moments when someone says, I'm going to do this, no matter what. And they rose to their feet to cheer him on. When Moussambani reached the end of the pool—50 meters—he made the speed turn he'd learned just days before. By the time he finished, thrashing at the water the entire way, he'd been in the pool nearly two minutes, more than double the world record time in the event. Moussambani received a standing ovation after touching the wall. "I send hugs and kisses to the crowd," Moussambani said. "They kept me going."

New York, New York

September 21, 2001
Mets vs. Braves

"What we're doing is the simplest thing of all," said Mets manager Bobby Valentine of the first baseball game played in New York after 9/11. "We are fighting fear in the name of freedom." Mets players and umps alike donned FDNY, NYPD, and Port Authority Police caps. During a 21-gun salute, the stadium was as silent as any stadium anywhere has ever been, and during the seventh-inning stretch, Liza Minnelli belted out her trademark "New York, New York." The fans, 41,235 of them, came to forget—or maybe to remember the way it was before that horrible day. "It felt like a piece of my insides were ripped out after last week," said Mets reliever and team captain John Franco, a lifelong New Yorker. "But this is good for the city. A couple of firefighters talked to me and told me that they were happy to see us playing ball again. It helped them to get away and just watch baseball for a few hours." The Mets beat the Braves 3-2 on a game-winning dinger by Mike Piazza.

One-Handed Wonder

September 22, 2002
Oronde Gadsden

In a blowout in which the Dolphins beat the
Jets 30-3, the most amazing play didn't result
in any points. Nevertheless, to call Oronde
Gadsden's one-handed snag for a first down
late in the first half acrobatic would be to
give too much credit to acrobats. Gadsden
celebrated the victory by waving a "What
Jinx? 1-0" sign as he exited the field. Later
he said, "I hadn't beaten them since I've been
here. That's four years. That's kind of rough."

Big Play in the Big House

September 24, 1994
Kordell Stewart to Michael Westbrook

After the game, University of Colorado coach Bill McCartney said simply, "I didn't think he could throw that far." The "he" was his quarterback, Kordell Stewart. And the throw—well, the throw was Herculean, covering 70 yards in the air as time expired in a game against Michigan. The 100,000-plus fans who converge on Ann Arbor for the Wolverines' home games watched the ball flutter across the sky, safe in the knowledge that all their team had to do was bat the ball down and they'd walk off with a victory. As the ball reached the 2-yard line, bodies went skyward and the first fingers to reach it belonged to Blake Anderson, a Colorado receiver. But Anderson didn't try to catch it—he wasn't supposed to. Instead, he swatted the ball toward the end zone, where teammate Michael Westbrook snagged it and fell to the ground. Final score: Colorado 27, Michigan 26. "Never give up," Westbrook shouted toward the sky. "Never give up."

The Grandest Slam?

September 25, 2000
Vince Carter

The basketball highlight of the Sydney Olympics: Vince Carter steals an errant pass, takes off just outside of the paint, scissors his legs in midair, and sails over 7'2" French center Frederic Weis to throw down what some dunkologists say was the most mind-boggling stuff in hoops history. "I don't have time to worry about who's there," Carter said. "I just put the ball in the hole." Said Team USA coach Rudy Tomjanovich: "The only time I've ever seen a play like that is when I jumped over my 4-year-old son on one of those Nerf ball baskets." Team USA beat France in the preliminary game, 106-94, and would beat them again in the final.

Remembering How to Win

September 26, 1998
Prairie View A&M vs. Langston University

Nine years. I-AA Prairie View A&M lost 80 straight football games. They were 0 for the '90s, and then some. Finally, though, that painful streak seemed to be coming to an end. Prairie View had a 14-6 lead over Langston University, an NAIA team, and time was running out in the fourth quarter. But then, with 34 seconds left on the clock, Langston cut Prairie View's lead to 14-12 on a 51-yard touchdown pass. Could Prairie View's defense stop the two-point try? Sure, a tie would be better than that other thing, but Prairie View desperately, desperately needed a W. And they got it: the Langston QB was dumped on an attempted keeper. *Prairie View wins! Prairie View wins! Prairie View wins!*

Mob Scene

September 26, 1999
Justin Leonard

The United States team trailed Europe 10-6 as the final day of the Ryder Cup matches began at The Country Club in Brookline, Mass. But what had the makings of a cakewalk for the Euros turned into a death march. The Americans, feeding off the energy of the partisan crowds, swept the first six matches, wiping out the deficit and seizing the lead. The match to determine the winner of the Cup turned out to be Justin Leonard against Spain's José María Olazábal. Down four holes with seven to play, Leonard won four holes (and split another), so the match was all square when the two arrived at the 17th green. Team USA had 14 points in hand—an assured tie—but needed half a point for the win. Leonard lined up a sharply breaking 45-foot putt for birdie and calmly stroked it in. When it dropped, most of the American team stormed the 17th green and piled on top of Leonard. It made for great TV, but it was lousy golf decorum: Olazábal could still tie the hole with his own putt for birdie. When the commotion finally subsided, a rattled Olazábal narrowly missed from 25 feet. "What happened on No. 17 was unfortunate, but I'm not going to apologize for being excited," said Tom Lehman, one of those who mobbed Leonard. "It was a great day for the American team." But a terrible day for American sportsmanship.

Trapping the Bear

September 27, 2000
Rulon Gardner vs. Alexander Karelin

Alexander Karelin was the Russian bear personified. The Greco-Roman wrestler tipped the scales at a massive 286 pounds and hadn't lost a match in 13 years. The real mindblower about Karelin's record, however, was that in the last 10 years he had ceded just a *single point*! Rulon Gardner, his American foe in the final at the Sydney Olympics, was a supersize farm boy from Wyoming. In their only previous meeting, three years earlier, Karelin had crushed him. This time, after a scoreless first round, Gardner's tactic of pressing against the Russian to prevent him from pulling off his signature move—the Karelin lift—paid off when Karelin unclenched his hold, giving Gardner a point under Greco-Roman rules. The point was enough to win the match. "I didn't think I could beat him. But I grew up on a farm, where you just go forward and get the job done," Gardner said. "Even though I wasn't thinking I was going to win, I was going to work as hard as I could."

Sleight of Hand

September 28, 2005
Ronnie Belliard

In a 1-0 loss to Tampa Bay during a tight
pennant race, Cleveland's Ronnie Belliard made
a play worthy of a win. In the seventh, with
a man on and one out, the Indians' second
baseman made a diving stab of a hot Aubrey
Huff grounder in the grass behind second base.
As Belliard was rolling over with his back
to second base, he flipped the ball over his
shoulder without looking to shortstop Jhonny
Peralta, who tagged the bag to get the force.
When a teammate said after the game that
it was the best play he'd ever seen, a grim
Belliard responded, "For me, right now, that
play don't mean nothing. We lost."

Say Hey!

September 29, 1954
Willie Mays

Shameless ESPN Classic Plug No. 4: At the crack
of Vic Wertz's bat, Willie Mays raced back, deep
into the vast centerfield of the Polo Grounds.
With barely a glance up, he reached out and,
incredibly, made the catch. Sorry, make that The
Catch. The greatest grab of all time? Even in a
book crammed full of 'em, we're saying it was.

Fleet of Foot

September 29, 1988
Florence Griffith-Joyner

It's the rare Olympian who can set a world record and then shatter it 100 minutes later. But we're talking about FloJo here. Florence Griffith Joyner's first world record came in the 200-meter semifinal at the Seoul Olympics: 21.56 seconds. But that wasn't all: in the final, FloJo ran a 21.34 200 meters and smiled through the finish line. No woman has touched that time since, nor has anyone approached her 100-meter record. "10.49. 21.34," Marion Jones said in 2004. "Those are the times that I strive for." You and many sprinters to come, Marion.

It Ain't Over 'til It's Over

September 30, 2002
Ravens vs. Broncos

The Denver Broncos probably figured, What the hell? They were losing 24-3 as the first half expired, so why not have kicker Jason Elam try a 57-yard field goal on the last play before heading to the locker room? Elam missed and Baltimore Ravens DB, Chris McAlister, caught the ball in the end zone. At first, it looked as if McAlister was just going to stand and wait for the final couple of seconds to tick off the clock. But suddenly he took off. With the Broncos and his own teammates shuffling around the field, most of them unaware that McAlister was headed upfield, the Ravens corner took the ball 107 yards for six more points. Said McAlister of his epic run: "All I saw was purple jerseys and open field until I hit the end zone."

October

Wild Ending

October 3, 1999
Mets vs. Pirates

The New York Mets needed a miracle. They were two games out of a wild-card berth with just three games to play. For weeks, Mets fans had stayed up late to get the West Coast scores, hoping for a loss here or a win there that would boost their team. Then, the cards started falling their way. The right teams lost, and the season's final game found them tied 1-1 with the Pittsburgh Pirates in the ninth. With one out, Mets outfielder Melvin Mora delivered a single; an Edgardo Alfonzo single and a John Olerud walk moved him along to third. Then, in the blink of an eye, it was over. With Mike Piazza at the plate, Brad Clontz threw a wild pitch and Mora took off to score the winning run standing up. The victory set up a one-game playoff win over the Reds, but the Mets eventually lost to the Braves in a memorable NLCS, four games to two. As miracles go, though, it had a pretty good run.

The Thrill Is Back

October 4, 1989
Will Clark

Chicago Cubs fans are accustomed to having their hearts ripped out and stomped on, but it usually takes a whole opposing team to do it. In Game 1 of the NLCS against the Giants, just one guy—sweet-swinging first baseman Will "The Thrill" Clark—bludgeoned the Cubbies into submission pretty much all by himself. Clark reached base five times, scored four runs, and drove in six. Four of those RBIs came on a grand slam in the fourth, which followed an RBI double in the first and a solo homer in the third. The final score was 11-3. "What did I think of Clark's performance?" asked Cubs skip Don Zimmer. "He had a hell of a week tonight."

Hail to the New King

October 5, 2001
Barry Bonds

Just three years after Mark McGwire shattered Roger Maris' 37-year-old single-season homer record of 61 and went on to set the new mark at 70, San Francisco's Barry Bonds ripped a first-inning homer against the Dodgers to relegate McGwire to second best. A few innings later, Bonds popped No. 72. And he wasn't quite done for the season ...

Fly Pattern

October 6, 2002
Priest Holmes

Priest Holmes normally keeps his feet on the ground. It makes it easier for the Kansas City Chiefs running back to run around or through people, which he is very good at doing. (Just ask the New York Jets. He'd been doing that to them all day.) But sometimes you need to try something a little different. Behind 25-22 and on the Jets' 19 with :27 remaining, the Chiefs sent in four wideouts to force man-to-man coverage. Holmes stayed at home to protect, but when the Jets didn't blitz, he slipped out the side door to catch a pass from QB Trent Green. Holmes first shook Jets LB James Darling like a martini. Then, when Jets DB Aaron Beasley set himself between Holmes and the goal line, Priest tried that something-a-little-different thing: he hurdled over Beasley into the end zone. "He would have got in anyway, even if he didn't jump," said Chiefs guard Brian Waters. "You're not going to see one guy stop him."

An Act of Sweetness

October 7, 1984
Walter Payton

Every other running back who ever carried the rock in the NFL ran in the shadow of Jim Brown and his 12,312 career yards. But Walter Payton wasn't every other running back, and when he took a toss in the third quarter of a Bears-Saints game at Soldier Field and ran off the left side for six yards, he topped Brown's record. Sweetness finished the day with 154 yards, and in doing so, shattered another Brown record: it was Payton's 59th career 100-plus-yard day, one better than Brown's career total.

Whole Lotta Shakin' Goin' On

October 8, 1988
LSU vs. Auburn

It was a classic example of SEC smashmouth ball, with the LSU and Auburn defenses fully controlling the game in Baton Rouge. The Tigers—the ones from Auburn, that is—came into the game ranked fourth in the country with a 4–0 record. LSU was a so-so 2–2. Trailing 6-0 with six minutes left in the game and the ball on their own 25, the Tigers—the ones from LSU, that is—looked like they would soon be 2-3. But Tommy Hodson, a junior QB with a world of talent who'd been expected to lift LSU to glory, finally did. Hodson moved LSU down the field as the noise in his home stadium swelled with each play. On fourth and nine from the Auburn 20, he hit Willie Williams for the first down and the frenzy heightened. But then the other Tigers dug in: three plays, not even a yard. With 1:41 left in the game and his team facing fourth and 10, Hodson found RB Eddie Fuller deep in the end zone. "That touchdown pass was the only throw I had left in me," Hodson said later. This time, the crowd yelled so loud the stadium rocked—literally. Turns out its vibrations were picked up on the LSU geology department's seismograph. The extra point made it 7-6 and the LSU defense held firm for the win.

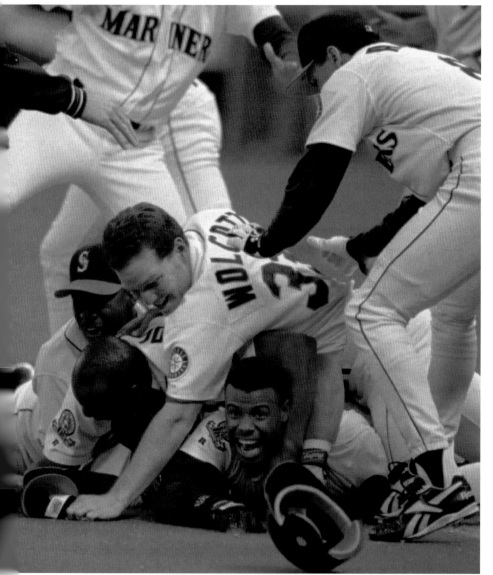

Yankees Winless in Seattle

October 8, 1995
Mariners vs. Yankees

The Yankees flew to Seattle eager to sew up the ALDS they were already leading two games to none. The Mariners had some Yankee-humbling tricks up their sleeves, though, taking the first two games at the Kingdome. The deciding Game 5 was tied 4-4 in the ninth when Seattle skipper Lou Piniella sent in Randy Johnson as a reliever (!). But the Big Unit gave up a run in the top of the 11th, setting the stage for Seattle's Edgar Martinez's game-winner in the bottom of the frame, a double that brought in Joey Cora and Ken Griffey Jr.

Reach Out and Touch

October 9, 1996
Jeffrey Maier

The Yankees had been denied entry to the ALCS a year earlier (*see* October 8, 1995), and when they finally did get in, it took a little help from a friend to win the first game. Trailing the Orioles 4-3 in the bottom of the eighth, Yanks shortstop Derek Jeter lifted one toward the seats in rightfield. But the ball didn't have quite enough pop on it, and the O's Tony Tarasco backed up to the wall and waited for it to plop into his glove. The ball never made it there, though, because one Jeffrey Maier, a 12-year-old kid from New Jersey, reached his glove out and flicked the ball into the stands. Replays showed that the ball would have either hit near the top of the fence or Tarasco would have caught it. "It was like a magic trick," said Tarasco. "I was getting ready to catch it, and suddenly, a glove appeared and the ball disappeared." The umps didn't see it that way. They ruled it a homer and the game went into extra innings. Yanks centerfielder Bernie Williams hit a solo shot in the 11th to give his team the win, 5-4.

Let's Play Two

October 9, 2005
Astros vs. Braves

In quite possibly the strangest game in postseason history, Houston's Roger Clemens recorded a 7-6 win over Atlanta in Game 4 of the NLDS after pitching just three innings. In relief. The Astros' Chris Burke won it with a walk-off, game-ending, series-ending homer. In the 18th inning. The Braves had 75 appearances at the plate. Houston had 65. A total of 42 players took part in the marathon. There were two grand slams. There was a homer in the bottom of the ninth to send the game into extra ... ah, make that into a whole new game. Combined, the two nine-inning tussles lasted nearly six hours. From the last out in the 10th until there was one out in the 18th, Houston went 21 official at-bats without a hit. Atlanta's Chipper Jones summed it all up when he said of his eighth plate appearance in the game, "My bat felt a little heavy."

Charlie Muscle

October 11, 1980
Pete Rose vs. Bruce Bochy

In Game 4 of the NLCS, the Phillies and the Astros were tied 3-3 in the top of the 10th. With Pete Rose on first, Phillies manager Dallas Green sent up slugger Greg Luzinski to pinch-hit. The Bull ripped a double into the leftfield corner, and that was all Rose needed. Building up a head of steam as he rounded second, he never gave a thought to stopping at third. Maybe he should have, because the ball got to Astros catcher Bruce Bochy well ahead of Pete. Taking dead aim, Rose plowed into Bochy shoulder-first and knocked the ball loose and Bochy almost into the stands. Phillies 5, Braves 3.

Legend of the Fall

October 11, 2003
Pedro Martinez vs. Don Zimmer

Boston's Pedro Martinez had thumped Karím García earlier in Game 3 of the ALCS, so Red Sox slugger Manny Ramirez had to know when he came to the plate in the fourth inning that Roger Clemens had him on his radar. Sure enough, The Rocket fired an inside fastball bearing purpose as well as mustard. The pitch didn't hit Ramirez, but he got the message and made for the mound anyway. The ensuing bench-clearing melee gave us one indelible image: a 72-year-old man ready to sacrifice his rotund body in defense of Yankee honor. Bench coach Don Zimmer charged Martinez, the pitcher sidestepped him, grabbed Zim's head, and heaved him to the ground. With the exception of his pride, Zimmer was pretty much unharmed. Better, the Yanks won 4-3 and went on to win the series in seven.

The Best Defense Is a Good Offense

October 12, 1986
Dave Henderson

For Dave Henderson, Game 5 of the ALCS was shaping up into a nightmare that might haunt him a good long time. The Red Sox centerfielder had scaled the fence in the sixth to catch a deep drive by Angels second baseman Bobby Grich, only to watch in horror as the ball popped out of his glove and over the wall, giving Grich a home run and the Angels the lead. But a chance for redemption presented itself in the ninth, when Henderson came to bat with the Sox trailing 5-4 and Rich Gedman on base. Hendu worked the count to 2-2, then got a forkball from Angels pitcher Donnie Moore that had payback written between the seams. "When I hit it I knew it was gone," Henderson said afterward. The Angels rallied to tie the game and send it into extra innings, but Henderson came through for the Sox again in the 11th with a sac fly to win the game, 7-6.

System Redundancy

October 13, 2001
Derek Jeter to Jorge Posada

It was all instinct. When Yankees shortstop Derek Jeter saw rightfielder Shane Spencer digging a ball out of the corner in Game 3 of the ALDS, he moved without thinking to back up the second cutoff man, first baseman Tino Martinez. Spencer launched a rocket that sailed over the heads of second baseman Alfonso Soriano and Martinez as the A's Jeremy Giambi chugged toward home with the tying run. But there was Jeter—the shortstop!—springing into action along the first baseline. Jeter grabbed the ball and shoveled a backhand throw to catcher Jorge Posada, who slapped the tag on Giambi. The Yanks held on to win 1-0. "That's my job on a ball in the corner," Jeter said with a shrug after the game. If it was, he was the only one who knew it.

Snatching Defeat from the Jaws of Victory

October 14, 2003
Steve Bartman

The Cubs were finally going to the World Series! Yes, for the first time since 1945, the Wrigley Field faithful would get their just reward. Up three games to two over the Marlins in the NLCS, and carrying a 3-0 lead heading into the top of the eighth, the Cubbies were set to ride the powerful right arm of Mark Prior straight into glory. Just six measly outs and all would be right in the world. Prior got the first of those six outs, then gave up a hit, then threw a pitch that was popped up and drifting toward the stands on the leftfield line. Moises Alou leaped for what would have been a great, in-the-stands catch for out No. 2. The catch, however, was foiled by Cubs fan Steve Bartman, who tried to snag a memento from the big night—and quickly earned infamy in Chicago akin to that of Mrs. O'Leary's cow. Fellow fans were furious and taunted Bartman, who was ushered to safety by security. Amid Wrigley's shocked quiet, the Cubs and Prior came unraveled: hits were given up, errors were made, and the Cubs generally played like the Cubs, allowing eight Marlins to cross the plate in the inning. To put the matter to rest, they lost Game 7, too.

Limping into Baseball History

October 15, 1988
Kirk Gibson

The guy can barely walk. How's he going to swing the bat? And if he does hit the ball, who's going to carry him to first base? Forgive Dodgers fans for thinking something like that with the A's leading 4-3 in Game 1 of the World Series. It was the bottom of the ninth inning, there were two outs, and as Kirk Gibson hobbled to the plate to pinch-hit with one man on against ace A's closer Dennis Eckersley, he looked like Walter Brennan on cortisone gimping to the plate. Gibson, nursing a sprained ligament in his right knee and a pulled hamstring in his left leg, worked Eckersley to a full count. Then Eck made a mistake, leaving a pitch out over the plate in Gibbie's zone. Gibson reached out and jerked a line drive into the rightfield stands. Dodgers Stadium went wild as a fist-pumping Walter Brennan circled the bases.

Irish Eyes Are Crying

October 15, 2005
USC vs. Notre Dame

The echoes of past glory and the promise of future thrills had been fully reawakened in South Bend with the arrival of coaching genius Charlie Weis. Now the green-jerseyed Irish were looking to lock down their resurrection with a win over top-ranked USC. Notre Dame was ahead 31-28 with less than a minute to go, but USC was knocking on the door at the Irish 2-yard line. With no timeouts remaining and only enough on the clock for one more play, USC quarterback Matt Leinart made a desperate dash for the end zone, just short of which he was jack-hammered by Irish LB Corey Mays. The ball squirted free and tumbled out of bounds, and— *Game over!*—Irish fans flooded the field. But as Lee Corso would say, "Not so fast, my friend." The officials huddled and ruled that the ball had gone out of bounds with seven seconds on the clock, and they spotted it on the Notre Dame 1, giving the Trojans one last go at it. Leinart kept the ball and was stuffed by the Irish surge, but as he spun to his left, he got a two-handed shove in the chest from Reggie Bush that sent him tumbling backward into the end zone for the win, 34-31.

Stolen Moment

October 17, 2004
Dave Roberts

It was as locked as locked can get. With a 3-0 lead in the ALCS, the Yankees held a 4-3 lead against the Red Sox in the bottom of the ninth inning of Game 4, and they had Mariano Rivera on the hill. When exactly does the World Series start? But then Rivera did something unusual: he walked Kevin Millar. Dave Roberts entered the game as a pinch-runner and started taunting Rivera, taking a huge lead off first. After he drew three throws, Roberts took off on a Rivera delivery to the plate and beat Jorge Posada's throw to second by a whisker. When Bill Mueller singled, Roberts sped around third, and slid home to score. The Red Sox triumphed 6-4 in 12 innings, the first win of four in a row that took them to the World Series.

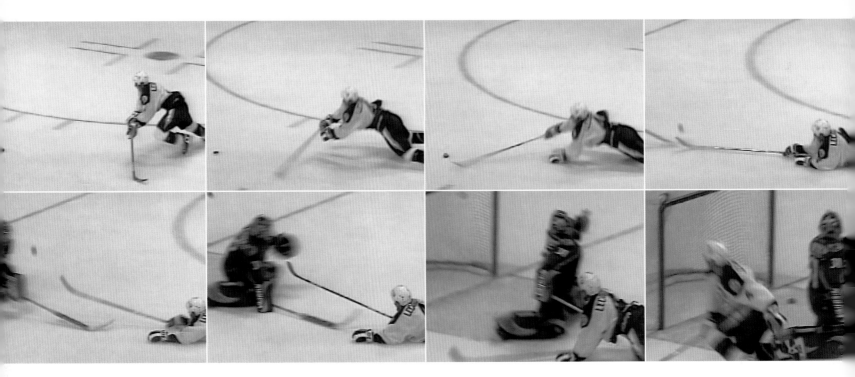

Stretching Drill

October 18, 2002
Vincent Lecavalier

Vincent Lecavalier darted into the clear, dove to the ice, raked the puck over the goalie's head and into the net, and hopped back on his feet, all in a single, fluid motion. Chris Berman made the call: "Vincent Lecavalier—*whoop!*—scores against *les Thrasherrrrs* of Atlanta." (Read with a French accent, *s'il vous plaît*.)

Blood and Guts

October 19, 2004
Curt Schilling

Still down to the Yankees 3-2 in the ALCS going into Game 6, Red Sox Nation badly needed a hero, and they got him in Curt Schilling, the beefy fireballer with a bad wheel. A day before the game, the Red Sox medics put sutures in Schilling's wounded ankle tendon. As the game wore on, blood seeped through Schilling's sock, the wound having opened up from the continual stress of pushing off the rubber. But the big man came through big time, holding the Yankees to one run. The Red Sox won 4-2 and forced the series to a Game 7 showdown.

Catch This If You Can

October 20, 1992
Devon White

The World Series between the Braves and the Blue Jays was tied at a game apiece and Game 3 was scoreless in the fourth when Atlanta's David Justice came to bat with Deion Sanders on second, Terry Pendleton on first, and nobody out. Justice launched a long, high drive to deep center. Toronto's Devon White took off at the crack of the bat, ran hell-for-leather to the wall, and made a jumping, twisting, back-to-the-infield snag as he smashed into the padding. "I guess it's just instinct," said White. "But I knew I had to get the ball fast to keep Deion from scoring from second. I'd be embarrassed if he scored all the way from second." Watching from the stands, former Cubs great Ernie Banks put the catch in historical context: "That would have been a tough catch for Willie Mays, DiMaggio, or Duke Snider."

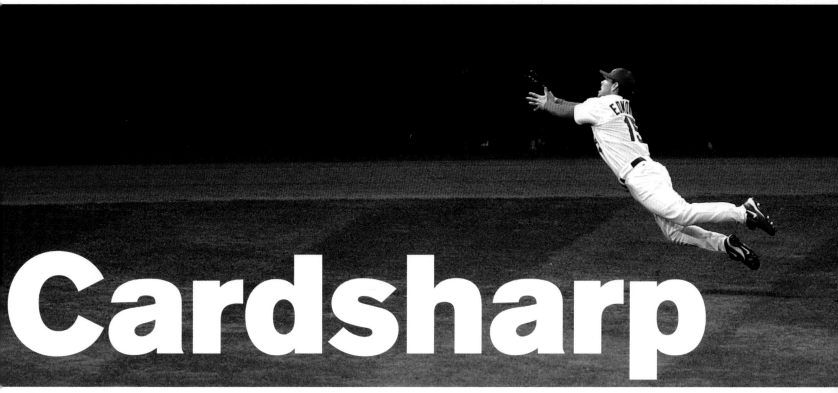

Cardsharp

October 21, 2004
Jim Edmonds

In Game 7 of the NLCS, with his team facing Roger Clemens and the Astros, Cardinals outfielder Jim Edmonds knew every run was critical. With Houston runners on first and second in the second inning, Brad Ausmus thumped one to deep center that seemed destined to drive in at least one run and possibly two. Your average centerfielder would have been focused on playing the ricochet off the wall, but Edmonds immediately broke straight for the ball, determined to haul it in. At the last possible second, he laid out like a wideout catching a sideline pattern and came up with it triumphantly. "I had to catch it," said Edmonds. "If I don't, we're in big trouble, down big-time." The Cards eventually lit up Clemens for a 5-2 win and headed to the World Series.

The Fisk Pole

October 21, 1975
Carlton Fisk

Shameless ESPN Classic Plug No. 5: Carlton Fisk was yelling. *Get over! Get over!* Boston was yelling. Everyone was yelling. (Though in Cincy it was a different yell.) In the bottom of the 12th inning of an epic Game 6 World Series battle with the Reds, Fisk launched one toward Fenway's Green Monster. The ball teased fans its entire flight, and as a nation held its breath, Fisk resorted to what announcers dubbed "body English." Perhaps due to his efforts, perhaps not, the ball smacked the foul pole—*fair!*—and the Sox won 7-6. To this day, Fisk's shot overshadows the 4-3 loss that came less than 24 hours later.

Score It E-1

October 22, 2000
Roger Clemens vs. Mike Piazza

Roger Clemens doesn't get paid for his fielding, but in the first inning of Game 2 of the World Series between the Yankees and the Mets, Clemens made a nice scoop of the jagged barrel of Mike Piazza's broken bat. But then The Rocket threw it well wide of first—actually, he threw it in what was later referred to as "the general direction of" the Mets catcher as Piazza ran toward first base. Clemens was fined $50,000.

Low and In, Up and Away

October 23, 1993
Joe Carter

No team since the 1977-78 Yankees had repeated as World Series champions, and if the Blue Jays were going to do it, they would have to overcome the Phillies' uncanny ability to play their way back into games they had no business being in. Having rallied from 5-1 down to take a 6-5 lead in the seventh inning, Philadelphia was looking to knot the Series at three games apiece. Phillies reliever Mitch "Wild Thing" Williams walked Rickey Henderson and surrendered a single to Paul Molitor. The next batter was Joe Carter, who worked Williams to 2-2 before Wild Thing let loose a low slider. "I'm definitely a low-ball hitter," said Carter after the game, a fact he made clear by sending the ball over the wall for a World Series-ending three-run homer. It was the first dinger to end a Series since Bill Mazeroski did it to the Yankees in 1960.

Jet Propulsion

October 23, 2000
Jets vs. Dolphins

Trailing the Dolphins 30-7 at the start of the fourth quarter of a Monday night game, the Jets launched a Vinny Testaverde-led rally that would become known as the Monday Night Miracle. The miracle began with this 30-yard TD to Laveranues Coles, and reached its most miraculous with a three-yard toss to tackle-eligible Jumbo Elliott with 42 seconds left. That one—Testaverde's fourth TD pass of the quarter—tied the game at 37-37 and sent it into overtime. It was left to Jets kicker John Hall to win the game 40-37 by piping a 40-yarder with 8:13 left in OT.

Blame It on Inexperience

October 24, 2002
Darren Baker

Giants manager Dusty Baker's three-year-old
son Darren took his job as team mascot and
bat boy seriously, and what's more serious
than the World Series? So when one of the
guys on Dad's team got a hit against the
Angels, Darren trotted out toward the plate
to collect the lumber. One big problem facing
the little guy: two Giants, J.T. Snow and
David Bell, were chugging toward the plate
with intent to score. What could have been
a calamity was averted when Snow deftly
scooped little Darren away to safety after he
had crossed the plate. "I saw the play unfold
and I was thinking about what my mom told
me," said manager Baker. "She said, 'He
shouldn't be out there—he's gonna get hurt.'"

One Consolation: 2004 Was Only 18 Years Away

October 25, 1986
Bill Buckner

The Red Sox were one out away from their first World Series title since 1918. The Mets had no one on and trailed by two runs in Game 6 of the World Series. Just when it looked like the long-suffering BoSox would finally have rings on their fingers, Gary Carter slapped a single for the Mets, and Kevin Mitchell and Ray Knight did the same. Then Bob Stanley threw a wild pitch that let the Mets tie the game. But the Red Sox seemed certain to escape calamity when Mookie Wilson hit a skittering grounder directly to veteran first baseman Bill Buckner. A simple scoop, an easy out, and all of New England could sigh with relief. But Buckner, whose knees had seen more miles than a Greyhound bus, let the ball dribble through his legs. Knight scored and the Mets won, then won again two nights later to take the Series.

The Umpire Strikes Out

October 26, 1985
Cardinals vs. Royals

The Cardinals, with a 1-0 lead over the Royals, were just three outs away from winning the World Series when things began to unravel. Why? Because of one of the worst calls—maybe *the* worst—in baseball history. Pinch-hitting for a pinch-hitter in a chess match between Cardinals manager Whitey Herzog and KC boss Dick Howser, the Royals' Jorge Orta tapped a pitch from reliever Todd Worrell weakly toward first. Jack Clark fielded it cleanly and flipped it to Worrell covering the bag. TV replays showed over and over and over again that Worrell had easily beaten Orta to the bag by as many as two steps, but first base umpire Don Denkinger called Orta safe. Rattled, St. Louis surrendered two runs and the game. Afterward, Herzog, had a few things to say: "The two best teams are supposed to be in the World Series. They ought to have the best umpires in it too. I think it's a disgrace. It's a joke. We haven't got one call from the three American League umpires in this thing. You want my opinion? It stinks. And we got that guy Denkinger behind the plate tomorrow. We got about as much chance of winning as a monkey." Whitey called it right—the Cardinals lost Game 7, 11-0.

Aces High

October 27, 1991
Jack Morris vs. John Smoltz

You always want your best pitcher on the mound when the World Series is on the line, and in Game 7 the Twins and the Braves both got what they wanted: Jack Morris for Minnesota, John Smoltz for Atlanta. Both aces got out of a few jams, but after eight innings, when Braves manager Bobby Cox pulled Smoltz, the score was 0-0. The score stayed that way and Morris stayed on the mound through the 10th, when his teammate Dan Gladden scored on a line drive by Gene Larkin over a drawn-in outfield. The gritty Morris, his era's ultimate money pitcher, was asked after the game how long he could have gone. His answer: "A hundred and twelve innings." Asked what it would've taken to get Morris out of the game, Twins skipper Tom Kelly said, "A shotgun."

"Now I Can Die in Peace"

October 27, 2004
Boston Red Sox

That's what diehard Red Sox fans—are there any other kind?—said in unison when Boston reliever Keith Foulke handled an easy comebacker and flipped the ball to Doug Mientkiewicz at first to complete a sweep of the Cardinals in the World Series. Foulke spoke for every New Englander dating back to John Smith when he said, "We did it. Now they can take that curse and stick it where the sun don't shine."

Tino Is Primo

October 31, 2001
Tino Martinez

The Yankees were down to their last out in Game 4 of the World Series when first baseman Tino Martinez dug in at the plate against Diamondbacks reliever Byung-Hyun Kim. Martinez, with his team two runs down and a runner on base, promptly bashed a game-tying homer that was postseason drama at its finest. As Martinez stepped on home plate in Yankee Stadium, he thrust his fists into the air, then traded countless high fives with teammates before reappearing from the dugout for a curtain call. Derek Jeter won it for the Yankees 4-3 with a homer in the bottom of the 10th, and the Bombers were back in the fight. The D-Backs would eventually win the Series in seven (*see* November 4, 2001), but for one night in the Bronx, Tino was Primo.

November

Close, but No Cigar

November 2, 1995
Florida State vs. Virginia

Since joining the ACC in 1992, Florida State had ripped off 29 straight conference wins. Ranked No. 2 in the country, the Seminoles went to Charlottesville expecting to notch consecutive win No. 30 against 24th-ranked Virginia. Surprisingly, the Cavaliers led most of the game and were stubbornly holding on to a 33-28 lead when it appeared that FSU started working its usual magic. On the game's final play, from the Virginia 6-yard line, Florida State's Warrick Dunn took a direct snap from center, ran slalom right, and slashed through the Virginia D until he got inside the 1. But then he lost the ball just shy of the goal line as he was tackled by Adrian Burnim and Anthony Poindexter, at which point time expired. "It was close, but it just came up short," Dunn said. "I lost the ball on the way in. When I fell back on it, I was in the end zone. I thought I was in. It almost worked."

Dance with Who Brung Ya

November 3, 1990
Virginia vs. Georgia Tech

Behind the aerial circus of QB Shawn Moore to WR Herman Moore, UVA rose to No. 1 in the polls and looked to defend that spot against third-ranked Georgia Tech in the first battle in November between undefeated ACC squads. Twice the Cavs held 14-point leads, but with less than three minutes left in the game, they trailed the Yellow Jackets 38-35. Still, the relentless Virginia offense, which had already racked up more than 500 yards, seemed poised to snatch the game away. With 2:44 left, Shawn Moore hit tight end Aaron Mundy with a quick pass from the 1 for what appeared to be the go-ahead score. Hold it! A flag on the play: illegal procedure. On the next play, a toss to Herman Moore was batted away. That left Virginia coach George Welsh with a decision: go for it on fourth and goal from the six or try to kick a tying field goal. After the game, Welsh defended his decision to go for three: "I still don't think that you try for a touchdown. My God, what are the chances of that?" Maybe not great, coach, but when you settle, make sure you settle for a *tie*. In the next two minutes and change, Tech QB Shawn Jones guided his team easily down the field to set up the game-winning field goal by Scott Sisson from 37 yards with :07 to play. Georgia Tech 41, Virginia 38.

The Bloop Heard Round the World

November 4, 2001
Luis Gonzalez

Bottom of the ninth of Game 7 of the World Series, Yankees up 2-1 over the Diamondbacks, Mariano Rivera (23 straight postseason saves) has the ball. Here's what's supposed to happen: you send somebody back to the clubhouse to make sure the champagne's ready. What actually happened? With a man on first, Rivera fielded a sacrifice bunt and threw wide of Derek Jeter at second, putting the tying run on second and the go-ahead on first. A Tony Womack double brought the tying run home, and then Luis Gonzalez, who swatted 57 home runs and drove in 142 runs during the regular season, stepped in to swing for the ... blooper. "That's the first time I choked up all year," said Gonzalez. "I knew the infield was playing in and I didn't have to try to hit it hard, just loop something out there and get the ball into play." His soft single fell in centerfield and Jay Bell coasted in with the game-winning run. Just like that, the Diamondbacks were World Champions.

Hey, Dad— Isn't That the Old Guy with the Grill?

November 5, 1994
George Foreman vs. Michael Moorer

You knew it wasn't a time warp or any sci-fi thing, because George Foreman was at least 30 pounds heavier than when he lost the Rumble in the Jungle to Ali a couple of decades before. But there he was, at 45, decked out in the same red trunks he wore in Zaire, fighting for a heavyweight title. His opponent: previously undefeated heavyweight champion Michael Moorer, 26. Win, lose, or draw, the exposure was sure to boost Foreman's ministry, mufflers, and meat-cooking hardware. But nobody expected what happened in the 10th, when Big George capped a flurry with a huge right hand that left Moorer, who was way ahead on all the judges' cards, on the canvas. Foreman, who had left boxing in 1977 when he was 28, became—and remains—the oldest fighter to win a title in any weight class.

Excuse Me, Zo—You're in My Way

November 7, 2005
Vince Carter vs. Alonzo Mourning

In the course of human events, every once in awhile a highlight comes along on *SportsCenter* that causes the entire nation of fans to flip out. Such was the case after this early November contest between Vince Carter's Nets and Alonzo Mourning's Heat. Carter snagged a rebound that was heading out of bounds, took a quick step around a defender as he dribbled behind his back, and drove toward the basket. Mourning jumped to block the shot, but Carter pushed the big man out of the way—forcefully, in midair—as he pinwheeled the dunk. As Carter fell back to the ground, a grateful nation hit rewind.

Big Red Miracle

November 8, 1997
Scott Frost to Shevin Wiggins to Matt Davison

Historically, the Nebraska Cornhuskers are more accustomed to running the football than throwing it. That might help explain why it took a miracle Nebraska catch to force overtime against Missouri. With 12 seconds left in the game and the Huskers trailing the Tigers 38-31, Big Red QB Scott Frost fired a 12-yard pass to Shevin Wiggins in the end zone. It was right on the numbers, but a Missouri defender was all over Wiggins and he couldn't hang on. A funny thing happened on the ball's way to the grass, though: it hit Wiggins' right foot and bounced back into the air, to be scooped up by Nebraska's diving Matt Davison. The miracle grab sent the game into OT, where the Huskers took control, going up 45-38 on their first drive and keeping the Tigers scoreless.

Well Armed

November 8, 1999
Emmitt Smith

Some people were beginning to talk about Cowboys running back Emmitt Smith retiring, but Vikings linebacker Ed McDaniel wasn't one of them. In the middle of what became a 63-yard touchdown run, McDaniel attempted to tackle Smith, only to wind up on the receiving end of one of Smith's great stiff-arms. Smith went on to split another pair of Minny defenders as well, to push Dallas to a 10-0 lead. Dallas would eventually lose 27-17, after Smith broke his right hand. Plausible though it might seem, there's no evidence that he weakened it with the stiff-arm.

Looks Like We Better Cancel the Party

November 9, 2002
LSU vs. Kentucky

Wildcats don't ordinarily stand much of a chance against Tigers, even on their home turf. So when Kentucky had powerhouse LSU down 30-27 with two seconds left in the game and the Tigers on their own 25, the party started. Kentucky coach Guy Morriss received a Gatorade bath ... Kentucky fans pressed in around the field, ready to storm it and rip down the goalposts ... and fireworks exploded over the stadium. All the Wildcats had to do was stop the Tigers from going 75 yards in two seconds. How hard could that be? Did we mention fireworks were going off over the stadium? LSU QB Marcus Randall added to the show by heaving the ball as far as he could, and after it was tipped around a bit, including touches by a few Wildcat fingers, the pigskin was grabbed by Tiger wideout Devery Henderson, who took it straight to the house. Touchdown LSU! Nightmare Kentucky!

No Way That Happened.
Absolutely No Way!

November 10, 1984
Maryland vs. Miami

The outlook wasn't pretty for the Maryland side that day. They were on the wrong side of 31-0 against Miami with just one half to play. But evidently no one told Frank Reich, the backup Terp QB, that Miami had an overwhelming D. So Reich did what anyone in his position would do: he led six drives down the field and posted 42 points. And when the Canes later came back and went for two to tie it, defensive back Keeta Covington whomped RB Melvin Bratton and said, "I think not." When the shouting died down and there were no more snaps to play, the biggest comeback in the history of NCAA Division I-A was complete: Maryland 42, Miami 40.

Pluck of the Irish

November 13, 1993
Notre Dame vs. Florida State

Florida State was the No. 1 team in the land as they faced off against Notre Dame, ranked No. 2, in South Bend. With just :51 left in the game and his team trailing 31-24, FSU's Charlie Ward started a drive from his own 37 and kept his team moving, until, with three seconds left in the game, the ball was on the Irish 14. On the sideline, FSU coach Bobby Bowden had already selected a play to go for two and win the game. But first he needed a TD. The Notre Dame rush forced Ward out of the pocket and to his left, where he threw toward the left side of the end zone. Two Noles receivers, Warrick Dunn and Kevin Knox, were in the area. But so was Irish cornerback Shawn Wooden, who jumped in front of the ball and swatted it to the turf as Notre Dame students rushed onto the field carrying a banner that read "Nobody Leaves #1." "I finally found out what the Big One is," said Bowden after the game. "It's the one you lose."

Hey, Miracles Happen

November 14, 1998
Tennessee vs. Arkansas

Down Tennessee way, the Volunteers were sniffing their first national championship since 1951. To the shock of the 106,000-plus who piled into Neyland Stadium to see Tennessee take on the 8-0 Arkansas Razorbacks, the boys in orange fell behind 21-3. The Vols managed to whittle the lead to 24-22 with 2:43 to go, but things still looked grim. At least they did until Hogs QB Clint Stoerner tripped over his own feet—untouched—and fumbled the ball away on the Tennessee 43. The Vols had trailed for more than 58 minutes when halfback Travis Henry pushed across the winning TD with :28 left in the game. "The only thing that saved us was a miracle," said UT guard Cosey Coleman. "That's the only way to explain it, because we pretty much had lost the game." The Vols went on to win the national championship.

Take All the Time You Need

November 15, 2004
Donovan McNabb to Todd Pinkston

The Cowboys D was so nonexistent against the Eagles in Dallas that it looked like they'd rather have been in Philadelphia. How bad *was* the Dallas D? On this second-quarter play, Donovan McNabb's jog away from the Dallas rush was nearly … casual. He had enough time to line up this 54-yard bomb to Todd Pinkston. After bringing it down at the Dallas 5, Pinkston gave the Cowboys defender a last push and strolled into the end zone to put Philly up 27-7. It would remain that kind of day for Dallas: final score, Eagles 49, Cowboys 21.

W-i-d-e Right!

November 16, 1991
Gerry Thomas

No. 1 Florida State vs. No. 2 Miami. Big rivals, both undefeated, both vying for the national championship. The Canes held a 17-16 lead with 25 seconds left to play, but walk-on FSU kicker Gerry Thomas, who'd already made three field goals on the day, had merely to make a fourth, from 34 yards, to send the home crowd into a flaming-spear-lovin' frenzy. Thomas missed right—and "Wide Right" became shorthand for FSU's habit of missing last-minute field goals.

Where Did That Ball Go?

November 17, 2001
Antuan Simmons

Chris Berman's call on Antuan Simmons' jaw-dropping INT that left UCLA's Brian Poli-Dixon scratching his head: "USC against UCLA—*whoop!*—between the legs for Antuan Simmons. He ... Could! ... Go! ... All! ... The! ... Way! ... with the pick. The Trojans over the UCLA Bruins, 27 to 0."

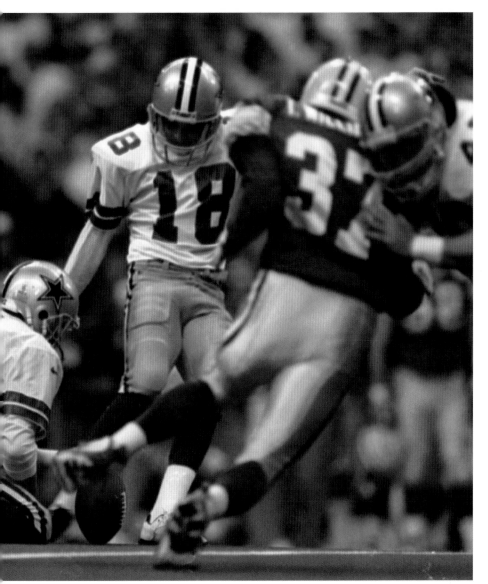

One-Man Show

November 18, 1996

Chris Boniol

This Monday night, Dallas kicker Chris Boniol proved that there's more than one way to put 21 points on the board. He recorded all of the Cowboys' points by booting a record-matching seven FGs in a 21-6 victory over the Green Bay Packers. Boniol's seventh score came after the Cowboys called timeout with 24 seconds left in the game, leading some to criticize the defending Super Bowl champs for piling on the points. "I wouldn't have been aware that he was close to the record unless the kicking coach told me," said Dallas coach Barry Switzer. And really, who can begrudge the Cowboys three measly points? Let the man kick.

Human Highlight Reel II

November 18, 2005
Dwyane Wade

Dominique Wilkins was the original Human Highlight Reel, but on this day, that title was passed to Miami's Dwyane Wade. In a 106-96 win over the Sixers, Wade had 9 rebounds, 10 assists, and 32 points—12 of them on dunks. The thumper that brought the crowd to its feet and made it onto every TV in the land was a thunderous alley-oop that made it look as if he had dropped from the rafters.

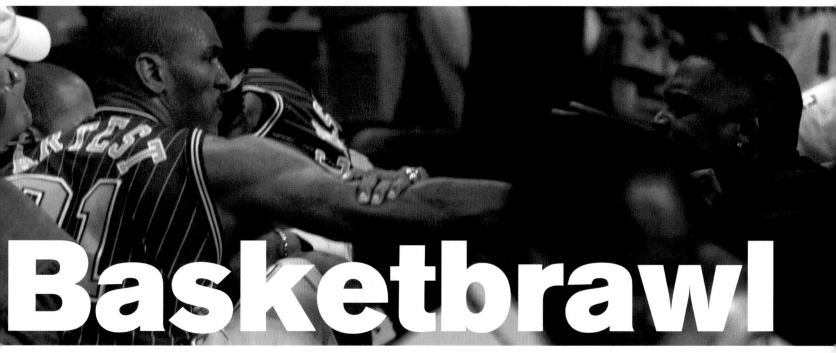

Basketbrawl

November 19, 2004
Pistons and Pacers

What started out as a friendly fistfight devolved into one of the worst brawls in sports history when Indiana's Ron Artest and Stephen Jackson went swinging into the stands. It began when Detroit's Ben Wallace was fouled by Artest on a drive to the hoop. Wallace turned and pushed Artest in the face. Things really went awry when a full cup of beer came out of the stands and hit Artest, who had lain down on the scorer's table. He jumped up and charged into the stands, throwing punches as he climbed over seats. Jackson followed, and the fans fought back. Officials stopped the game with 45.9 seconds remaining. "It's the ugliest thing I've seen as a coach or a player," said Pistons coach Larry Brown. Pacers coach Rick Carlisle concurred: "I felt like I was fighting for my life out there." The Pacers were showered with debris as they made for the locker room. A fan in a Pistons jersey approached Artest and shouted at him, so Artest punched him and dropped him. The Pacers' Jermaine O'Neal also cold-cocked a customer. "The events at last night's game were shocking, repulsive, and inexcusable," commissioner David Stern said the following day. "A humiliation for everyone associated with the NBA."

And the Band Played on

November 20, 1982
Cal vs. Stanford

Everybody's favorite marching-band play in college football history ended with California senior Kevin Moen dashing through the Stanford band like a bull running through the streets of Pamplona. Long forgotten now is the fact that, moments before, John Elway had led the Palo Altos down the field to a game-winning field goal. Or so it seemed. With four seconds left, Cal received the kick, and five laterals later, Moen found himself with only some tuba players and trumpeters blocking his way to the goal line. For the first time in history, the ultimate pickup line—"I'm with the band"—was rendered useless.

The Icing on the Cake

November 21, 1981
Marcus Allen

It was a heckuva year for USC's Marcus Allen. He won
the Heisman. He racked up eight games of 200-plus yards
rushing. And he set the NCAA single-season rushing mark.
But nothing could have made it sweeter than beating
them—UCLA—by scoring a touchdown with 2:14 left in the
game to put the Trojans ahead 22-21. Maybe even sweeter
was Trojans noseguard George Achica blocking a UCLA field
goal attempt as time disappeared from the clock, dashing
UCLA's Pac title and Rose Bowl hopes.

You Gotta Believe in Yourself

November 21, 1999
Corey Bradford

The Detroit Lions held a tenuous 17-12 lead over the Green Bay Packers' until Brett Favre put his team ahead for good by leading Corey Bradford to a spot in the end zone that only Bradford could reach—and only by making a lunging, one-handed snag for the TD. The Lions challenged the call, but it was upheld. "I always try to focus on the ball, and I brought it in and thought I caught it," Bradford said. "Anytime the other team asks for a replay, it makes you nervous, but I was positive I caught it." Take it easy, Corey, you caught it.

Coming Up Roses

November 22, 1997
Charles Woodson

Ohio State fans can be forgiven for thinking it was Desmond Howard all over again, but this time, it was Michigan defensive back and all-around menace Charles Woodson who put the worst hurt on them. With the Wolverines trying to finish off a perfect regular season, Woodson dropped back to his own 22 to field a punt, caught it, turned up the sideline, and saw nothing but daylight ahead of him. "It reminded me of Desmond Howard's return a few years ago," said Ohio State coach John Cooper, whose record against UM was unmentionable in Ohio. Michigan moved in front 20-0 and held on to win by six, in part thanks to an interception in the end zone to end an OSU threat by—who else?—Woodson. The victory helped put Michigan in the Rose Bowl, which they won, along with the national championship.

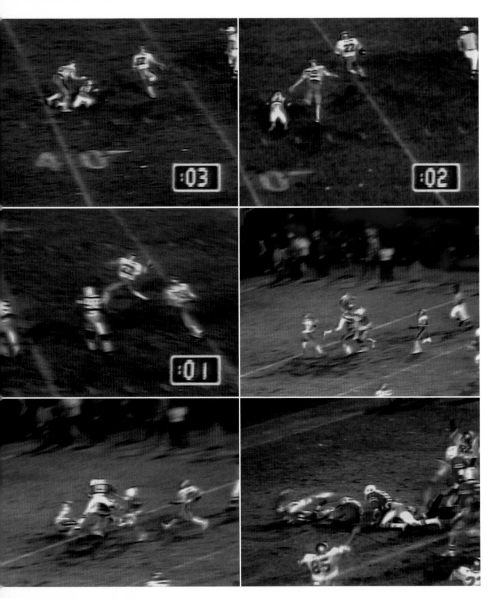

:03

:02

:01

Ask and Ye Shall Receive

November 23, 1984
Doug Flutie to Gerard Phelan

The game between Boston College and Miami had been the shoot out everyone expected it to be, what with Doug Flutie and Bernie Kosar behind center for their respective clubs. The muddy Orange Bowl field and dirty unis only enhanced the feel of a knockdown classic. There were only six seconds left in the game when Flutie took the final snap on the Miami 48. The tiny No. 22 scrambled for his life all the way to his own 37, then dashed to his right and let the ball fly 64 yards to his roommate at BC, wideout Gerard Phelan. "I didn't think he could throw the ball that far," said Phelan, who caught the ball at the 1-yard-line and tumbled backward into the end zone for a 47-45 BC win. "I honestly believed when we ran that play, we had a legitimate chance," said Flutie. "I'm not saying that I anticipated it happening, but I'm saying we had a chance, and that's all I ask for."

Not Just Any Other Game

November 23, 1991
Desmond Howard

In a 31-3 blowout of Ohio State, Michigan junior Desmond Howard rushed for eight yards and picked up 96 more on three catches. The play that put the lance through the heart of the Buckeyes faithful, however, was a 93-yard second-quarter punt return for six—the longest in Wolverines history. Howard split two hapless OSU tacklers at the 10 and shed another at the 18. Then he was off to the end zone, where he did his best imitation of the Heisman statue before being lost in a wave of his teammates. Howard won the actual trophy the following month. "I thought about fair-catching it because they were coming so fast," Howard said. "But I thought, This is the Ohio State game."

The Foot Is Quicker than the Eye

November 24, 2002
Brad Johnson to Joe Jurevicius

Upon returning to the game after having his eye checked for an injury, Tampa Bay's Brad Johnson got busy. With the Bucs trailing the Packers 7-6, Johnson took the field position presented to him by a Brian Kelly pick and engineered a mini drive to the Green Bay 4, where he threw a quick out to Joe Jurevicius that was an absolute laser beam. The receiver hauled it in but was ruled out of bounds. Bucs boss Jon Gruden threw out the challenge flag, and the call was overturned, sparking a 21-7 Tampa Bay win.

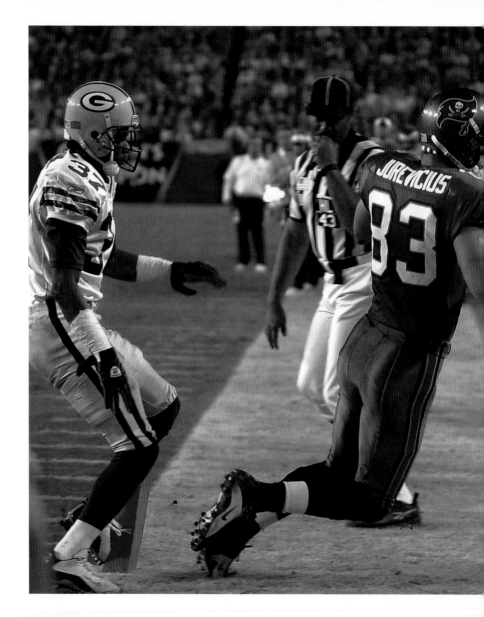

¡No Más! ¡No Más!

November 25, 1980
Sugar Ray Leonard vs. Roberto Durán

In a rematch for the welterweight title, the powerful Roberto Durán was expected to beat Sugar Ray Leonard once again. But this time, Sugar Ray's quick hands and sharp taunts left Durán unable to respond. With 16 seconds left in the eighth round, Durán turned away from Leonard and told the referee, "*¡No más! ¡No más!*" After the victory, Leonard said, "To make a Roberto Durán quit was better than knocking him out."

On the Receiving End

November 26, 1989
Flipper Anderson

The Rams played in LA back then, baby, and a guy named Willie "Flipper" Anderson was ready for prime time. With the Rams down 17-3 against the Saints with 2:46 to play, Flipper set up one TD with a 46-yard catch and scored another on one of his 15 catches on the day for a league record of 336 yards. To polish it off, Anderson made the catch that set up the winning field goal in overtime. On the whole, probably the best day ever for a guy named Flipper.

The Rally at Tallahassee

November 26, 1994
Florida State vs. Florida

FSU fans might have thought the other team from Florida was nicknamed the Elephants instead of the Gators, given the way they stomped all over the home boys at Doak Campbell while building a 31-3 fourth-quarter lead. But then Noles quarterback Danny Kanell got hotter than Tallahassee in August and lit up the Florida defense for 232 yards in the space of 13 minutes. Four TDs later, the game ended in a tie, FSU's score tying the Division I record for the largest fourth-quarter comeback. Gator fans remember the game as the Choke at Doak. Noles faithful prefer to think of it as the Rally at Tallahassee.

Angel in the End Zone

November 28, 2004
Ronald Curry

The Oakland Raiders rallied from 11 down to beat the Denver Broncos in the snow 25-24 in Mile High. The winning TD was set up by a 64-yard bomb from Kerry Collins to Ronald Curry. Indeed, it was Curry who made a spectacular one-handed catch in the back of the end zone on the previous Oakland possession to cut the Broncos' lead to 24-19. Curry didn't spike the ball or do the funky chicken when he scored. He celebrated in a style appropriate to the venue: he made a snow angel in the end zone.

A Legend Leaves the Field

November 29, 1997
Eddie Robinson

The last play of Grambling's 30-7 loss to Southern University marked the end of Coach Eddie Robinson's 57-year run at Grambling's helm, which included three undefeated seasons, 17 conference titles, and an NCAA-record 408 victories. (Only John Gagliardi of St. John's University has since surpassed that number.) Perhaps Robinson's most enduring legacy, though, is represented by the more than 200 players he coached who went on to play in the NFL. One of those players, Doug Williams, was the MVP of Super Bowl XXII and became Robinson's successor.

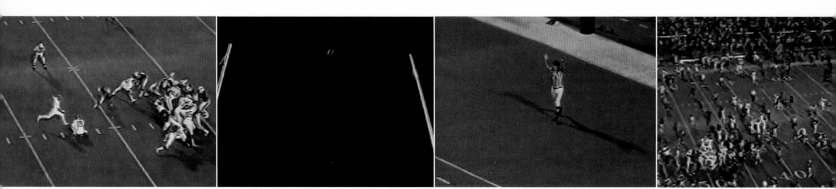

Iron Foot Wins Iron Bowl

November 30, 1985
Alabama vs. Auburn

College football doesn't get any better than the annual game between Alabama and Auburn, a.k.a. the Iron Bowl. In the 50th meeting of the two schools, the lead changed hands four times in the final 7:03. Bo Jackson was running wild for the Tigers, but every time it looked as if Auburn had won it, Bama fought back like a cornered animal. In the end, it was Tide kicker Van Tiffin who settled the score. As the clock expired, Tiffen split the posts from 52 yards out to give Alabama a 25-23 win in the most unforgettable Iron Bowl of them all. "This is why it's the greatest game in the country," Tide coach Ray Perkins said. Pretty big claim. But we'll allow it's right up there with Michigan-Ohio State, USC-UCLA, and Harvard-Yale.

December

Running Wild

December 1, 2002
Michael Vick

Everyone knew Michael Vick could run, they just didn't
know he could run like this. In a 30-24 overtime victory
over the Vikings, the Falcons QB picked up 173 yards
on just 10 carries, including a 46-yard TD romp to win
the game. Vick's rushing yardage broke the mark for a
quarterback in a single game, previously owned by Tobin
Rote, who racked up 150 back in 1951. Immediately after
the game, the Hall of Fame called and asked for Vick's
shoes. Falcons coach Dan Reeves said, "I've never seen
anyone turn on the jets like that."

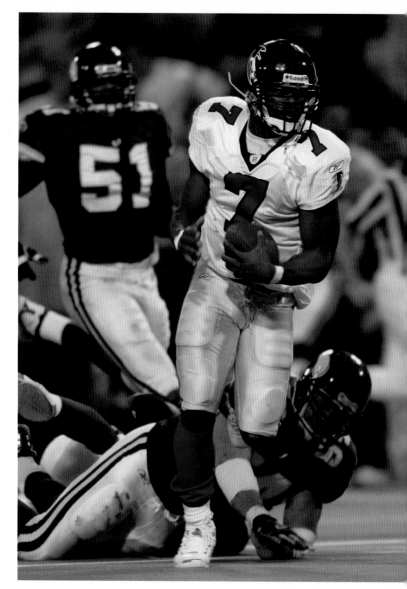

You Take It.
No, *You* Take It.
Are You Sure?

December 1, 2002
Bears vs. Packers

Chicago's Damon Moore picked off a Brett Favre pass late in the second quarter near his own end zone, and then both teams started with the slapstick. Moore brought the ball back to about his 40, but then coughed it up. Green Bay's Mike Flanagan picked it up in heavy traffic and tried a lateral, but the ball ended up in the hands of Roosevelt Williams of the Bears. For a moment it looked like Williams might Go! ... All! ... The! ... Way! ... but the Packers' Javon Walker saved a TD when he brought him down at the 13.

Almost Perfect

December 2, 1985
Bears vs. Dolphins

The Bears had been football's best squad all season long, and when December came with the team at 12-0, visions of an undefeated season began to dance in Windy City heads. The road to a perfect record went through Miami, though, and this routing produced the highest-rated *Monday Night Football* game in history. Dan Marino's Dolphins put up 31 points in the first half, scoring on each of their first five possessions. But it was the Miami D that really put the Bears off the scent, racking up six sacks and three interceptions. Even the first loss of the season couldn't lower the Bears' optimistic outlook. "I don't think it affects the achievements of the 1985 Bears," safety Gary Fencik said after the game. "We're not infallible." But the 38-24 loss was only a bump in the road. The Bears finished the regular season 15-1.

Gonna Fly Now

December 3, 2005
Reggie Bush

A perfect regular season for USC was punctuated with a 66-19 thrashing of crosstown rival UCLA. USC's Reggie Bush lifted the rout to legendary status by rushing for 260 yards and two touchdowns. In this second-quarter score, Bush took to the air, leaping directly over UCLA DB Marcus Cassel and into the corner of the end zone.

Show Us Something

December 3, 2005
Northwest Missouri State vs.
North Alabama

Northwest Missouri State trailed North Alabama, 24-19, with just 23 seconds left in an NCAA Division II playoff game—plenty of time for the guys from the Show Me State to show us something special. From three yards out, Northwest Missouri's Josh Lamberson found Raphael Robinson in the corner, and the Bearcats were heading to the title game against Grand Valley State.

Crossing the Language Barrier

December 4, 1988
Barry Sanders

Barry Sanders had won the Heisman just hours earlier, but the meaning of that on the other side of the Pacific could have lost something in translation. So in a Coca-Cola Bowl game played in Tokyo, the Oklahoma State junior demonstrated what the Heisman was all about. Sanders tore through the Texas Tech defense for 332 rushing yards and four touchdowns. The four scores put his season total at 39—10 more than anyone in history—and the yards helped him set a single-season NCAA rushing record of 2,628 yards. In a highlight-packed nail-biter, OSU edged Tech 45-42.

Gig 'em, Aggies

December 5, 1998
Kansas State vs. Texas A&M

The Texas A&M Aggies needed one more thrill in this double-overtime thriller if they wanted to scuttle the No. 2 Wildcats' shot at the national championship, but when A&M's Sirr Parker caught QB Branndon Stewart's pass, he was still 28 yards from home. Parker moved inside on K State cornerback Jerametrius Butler, then shot toward the opposite corner. There, with a desperate dive, he just grazed the orange goal marker. "I'm only 5'11", but I was 6 feet on that one," Parker said later. With the 36-33 win, A&M marred the Wildcats' until-then perfect season and reshuffled pretty much the entire Bowl Championship Series.

Talk About a Fast Start

December 5, 2004
Bethel Johnson

If you got caught in traffic and were a little late getting to your seat at the Patriots-Browns game, all you missed was the most exciting play of the day. Matter of fact, it was the key play as well. Hey, don't worry about it. Isn't that what highlights are all about? So here's what happened: New England's Bethel Johnson took the opening kickoff at his 7, headed straight up the field, cut right behind his blockers, found daylight down the right side and it stayed clear 'til the end zone. Turns out that Johnson's run set the tone for the rest of the game, a 42-15 Patriots blowout.

Same Old, Same Old

December 6, 1992
Jerry Rice

In a 49ers rout of the Dolphins, Jerry Rice broke Steve Largent's record of 100 TD catches in a career when he pulled down a 12-yarder from Steve Young with 8:56 left in the game. Rice was swarmed by teammates in the end zone and then ran off the field holding the ball aloft. "I've been chasing this for a long, long time," Rice said after the 27-3 Niners win. "It's a lot of pressure off me now. I can go out next week and relax."

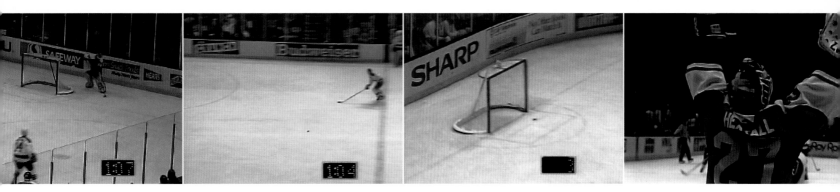

He Shoots!
He Scores!

December 8, 1987
Ron Hextall

He was known as the best stick-handler in pads and mask of his era, and when he became the first goalie to shoot and score a goal in an NHL game, Philly's Ron Hextall didn't play the surprised role very well. With 1:12 left and trailing 4-2, Boston pulled its goalie. Hextall gathered in the puck that had been dumped toward him, and with no one around, took his time lining up a shot. The puck landed near the Boston blue line and slid into the net, clearing the right pipe by about three inches. "I don't mean to sound cocky, but I knew I could do it," the goalie boasted later. "It was a matter of when."

Just Your Basic Tip Drill

December 9, 2001
Jeff Graham

Leaves, schmeaves. The real beauty of autumn comes every Sunday when we're treated to a Catch of the Day. On this afternoon the honor went to a grab by the San Diego Chargers' Jeff Graham. The wideout reached all the way over the shoulders of Eagles cornerback Troy Vincent for the Doug Flutie pass. He got enough of his hands on the ball to tip it back into the air. A few yards down the field, Graham grabbed the ball for keeps and took it home the last 40 yards. The effort tied the game at 7-7, but sometimes not even a Catch of the Day is enough. Final score: Eagles 24, Chargers 14.

His Net Runneth Over

December 9, 2001
Craig Johnson

LA Kings left wing Craig Johnson drove more than the puck past Blackhawks goalie Jocelyn Thibault. In a second-period power play against Chicago, Johnson went airborne at the same moment his shot went true. Half-falling, half-sliding—*whoop!*—Johnson joined Thibault in the net. It was the Kings' third goal in a game they'd take 5-2.

Road Warriors

December 10, 2004
James Madison vs. William & Mary

James Madison was looking to avenge a loss during the regular season to William & Mary when the two teams locked horns in the Division I-AA semifinals. JMU was also looking to nail down its third straight road win in the playoffs, something no other I-AA team had ever done. They accomplished both goals by turning four William & Mary turnovers into scores to win, 48-34.

The Greatest Calls It Quits

December 11, 1981
Muhammad Ali vs. Trevor Berbick

The end came for The Greatest in the Bahamas against Trevor Berbick, an undistinguished opponent who seemingly won nine of the 10 rounds. "You can't beat Father Time," Ali said in a whisper in his dressing room. "This was my last fight. I know it is. I'll never fight again. Berbick couldn't have beaten me if I wasn't 39 years old, but I am."

Over in a Snap

December 11, 1999
Mount Union vs. Rowan University

Mount Union, riding an NCAA-record 54-game winning streak, won the coin toss to start overtime in its Division III semifinal game against Rowan. Mount U decided to play D first, and Rowan's Jason Frabasile punched one in from seven yards out to give his team a 24-17 lead. With its streak in peril, Mount Union managed just five yards in three downs, and faced fourth and five. Quarterback Gary Smeck threw a hero ball to Jason Richards, who made a leaping grab, but Richards was hammered by three Rowan defenders as he came down and coughed up the ball, ending the game and the streak.

Plowed Over

December 12, 1982
Patriots vs. Dolphins

The unlikely hero of the New England Patriots' 3-0 win over the Dolphins was Mark Henderson, a convict on work release. His job? Drive the snowplow. On this near-blizzard day in Foxborough, the snow was piling up so fast, neither team could score. With 4:45 remaining, Patriots coach Ron Meyer called time and signaled for Henderson to use his snowplow to clear the yard markers—and swing in to quickly plow a place for John Smith to try a field goal. The 33-yard kick was good—and stayed good over the Dolphins' protests—as the crowd went wild for Henderson. In a post-game interview, Henderson had a strictly All-Pro response: "I just jumped on the tractor and went out there and cleared the path off."

Shooting Gallery

December 13, 1983
Pistons vs. Nuggets

The Pistons beat Denver 186-184 in triple OT, and the story here is in the numbers. Both teams broke the old mark of 173 for a team in a game (Boston, 1959), and the combined 370 topped the old mark of 337 (San Antonio vs. Milwaukee, 1982). Other digits that went in the books: 142 field goals made by both teams, and the 74 made by Detroit. John Long hit the game-winner for Detroit with 1:11 left in the third OT.

Better Late Than Never

December 15, 2002
Tennessee vs. Georgia Tech

Tennessee was trailing Georgia Tech by 13 with 7:25 left, but rallied to within 69-67 with less than a full tick remaining on the clock. The Vols had no timeouts left when Jon Higgins grabbed an inbounds pass, turned, and fired a half-court shot over the arms of Tech's Ismai'il Muhammad. "I just turned and shot it," Higgins said, "and it went in for us." It dropped for three. Final score: 70-69.

Football Interruptus

December 16, 2001
Cleveland Fans

Cleveland fans were on their feet when Browns quarterback Tim Couch hooked up on fourth down with wide receiver Quincy Morgan at the Jacksonville 9 for a first down with 1:08 remaining. Down 15-10, Couch & Co. were looking for a final-minute win, but up in the replay booth, officials had other ideas, even after Couch took a quick snap and spiked the ball to stop the clock at 48 seconds. The officials in the booth reversed a ruling on the field by determining that Morgan never had possession of the ball, thus turning the ball to the Jags on downs. Instantly, a cascade of beer bottles, cups, and assorted debris rained down on the field. "We were trying to finish the game, but as we lined up, a bottle zipped past my head," said the head official, Terry McAulay. "At that point I decided that it was just too dangerous to finish the game." The Jags' Jimmy Smith took hyperbole to a new level: "We feared for our lives ... It felt like I was starring in *Saving Private Ryan* or something." (Uh, Jimmy, the bottles were plastic.) Commissioner Paul Tagliabue got on the horn and instructed that the game be continued. Twenty-five minutes later, in a nearly empty stadium, Jaguars QB Mark Brunell took a knee twice and the game was officially over.

Take the Cavs, Give the 67 Points

December 17, 1991
Cavaliers vs. Heat

The Cavaliers led the Heat by 20 at halftime, a slim margin considering the final score was 148-80, the most lopsided in NBA history. "I don't know what we played, but it wasn't basketball," the Heat's Glen Rice said of the game. Eight Cleveland players scored at least 10 points—this pass from Steve Kerr set up two of Jimmy Oliver's 11. But, remarkably, no Cav reached 20.

A First Time for Everything

December 18, 2005
Steve Smith

With Carolina battling for first place in their division, Panthers wide receiver Steve Smith took an end-around play from 20 yards out and leaped over a pack of Saints for a TD that fueled a 27-10 Panthers victory. It was Smith's first career rushing touchdown.

A Big Night Out in New Jersey

December 20, 1983
Guy Lafleur and Steve Shutt

Pity the poor Devils. They got their horns handed to them by Montreal, 6-0. At home. And, to make the loss more memorable, Montreal's Guy Lafleur scored his 500th career goal—only the 10th player in NHL history to do so—and the Habs' Steve Shutt netted his 400th.

Sharing the Fun

December 21, 2003
Saints vs. Jaguars

The play was zany enough for Chris Berman to break out his best Curly imitation. With seven seconds left in the game and the Saints trailing the Jags 20-13, New Orleans' Aaron Brooks passed to Donte' Stallworth, who lateraled the ball to Michael Lewis, who pitched it out to Deuce McAllister, who tossed it to Jerome Pathon, who took it 21 yards and dove into the end zone for six. *Let's go to OT!* Not so fast. Remember, these are the Saints we're talking about. Sure enough, kicker John Carney missed the PAT. No OT required.

Rising to the Occasion

December 22, 1984
BYU vs. Michigan

BYU signal-caller Robbie Bosco went into the Holiday Bowl against Michigan with a lot on his mind: a win would sew up the national title for his team, and he had some sore ribs to boot. Midway through the first quarter, he forgot about those things for a moment when he was leveled on a late hit by the Wolverines' Mike Hammerstein and carried from the field. After Michigan took a 17-10 fourth quarter lead, Bosco came off the bench and took control of the game, albeit very gingerly. He limped and he shuffled, but at one point he ran 27 yards for a key first down. With 1:23 left in the game, Bosco hit Kelly Smith for his second touchdown pass of the quarter to put BYU ahead to stay, 24-17.

Playing Through Pain

December 22, 2003
Brett Favre

His dad, Irvin Favre, had died just the day
before, so Brett Favre honored him the best
way he knew how, by throwing for 399
yards and four TDs in a 41-7 Packers rout
of the Raiders. On just his fourth play from
scrimmage in the game, Favre connected with
Robert Ferguson for 47 yards. On the next
snap, Favre threw high to tight end Wesley
Walls, who made a towering leap and came
down with it in the back of the end zone for a
22-yard score.

The Immaculate Reception

December 23, 1973
Franco Harris

Shameless ESPN Classic Plug No. 6: It is the most astounding pass in NFL history. With 26 seconds to play, Steelers QB Terry Bradshaw fired a bullet, and wide-eyed rookie back Franco Harris watched fullback John "Frenchy" Fuqua get smashed by Raiders safety Jack Tatum. Harris tracked the ball's sharp backward deflection, planted his left foot, caught the ball on his shoelace, and ran in a go-ahead touchdown that eliminated the Raiders from the playoffs, 13-7. But did Fuqua touch the ball? Was his the last touch? The rules of the day stated that an offensive player—Harris—could not catch a pass that had been touched by a teammate unless a defensive player made contact with it between the touches. Fuqua maintains he knows what exactly transpired, but to this day, he's never told all.

David Slam Dunks Goliath

December 23, 1982
Chaminade vs. Virginia

Virginia was ranked the No. 1 team in the land, and with 7'4" Ralph Sampson in the pivot, they figured to stay there for a while. And Chaminade University? The tiny (800 students) Catholic liberal arts school in Honolulu had only had a basketball team for seven years. The Silverswords' expectations for their meeting with the top-ranked Cavs? "I felt if we lost by anything less than 20 points to them, I would be happy," admitted coach Merv Lopes later. They did a little better than that. In what's still considered the biggest upset in college basketball history, Chaminade beat Virginia 77-72. Virginia opened up a seven-point lead in the second half, but Chaminade ripped it away from them for good with 1:37 left in the game. Said a jubilant Lopes after the game: "I just told my guys they had nothing to lose, so go out there and play, that it was an honor for a school like Chaminade to play the No. 1 team in the nation." Beating them? Icing on the cake.

Great Leap Forward

December 25, 2004
Ben Troupe

Tennessee Titans rookie Ben Troupe was a tight end, not a high jumper, though a play he made against the Denver Broncos makes you wonder if he missed his calling. After an interception gave the Titans the ball with 12 seconds left in the half, Troupe snagged a short pass from quarterback Billy Volek and leaped over—*way* over—Denver cornerback Champ Bailey. The 15-yard gain set up a Titans field goal, the last Titans points in a 37-16 loss. Maybe Troupe should have kept on jumping.

All for Naught

December 27, 1991
Tim Hardaway

The good news for Golden State: the old deadeye, Chris Mullin, drained a three with :17 left to win a squeaker against the T-Wolves. The crazy news? Warriors point guard Tim Hardaway, who was averaging nearly 23 points per game, went 0 for 17 from the field, setting a new NBA mark—the old one was 0 for 15—for futility.

Super Mario Remembers How It's Done

December 27, 2000
Mario Lemieux

He was the owner, chairman, president, and chief executive officer of the Pittsburgh Penguins, and he hadn't laced up his skates for real in three and a half years. So when Mario Lemieux took the ice against Toronto, it was only normal for everyone watching to think he'd still be brilliant. Guess what? He was. Lemieux notched a goal and two assists in a 5-0 win for the Penguins. "I was a little surprised by the way I played," Lemieux said after the game, before which his retired jersey 66 had to be lowered from the rafters. Clearly, Lemieux was rusty—it took him all of 33 seconds on his first shift to post his first assist.

Dances with Wolverines

December 28, 2005
Nebraska vs. Michigan

Trailing 32-28 with only two seconds left in the Alamo Bowl against Nebraska, Michigan QB Chad Henne threw a short pass and then watched as his teammates performed a near-textbook-quality Keystone Kops series of laterals all over the field. The Wolverines almost got a touchdown out of the madness, but Nebraska's Titus Brothers and Zack Bowman finally spoiled their fun with a game-saving tackle. Now, if only the Michigan band had taken a page out of the Stanford band's playbook and marched out onto the field ...

Photography Credits

Action Images: 4/23/99, 7/1/90; Phil O'Conner, 7/7/90; AP Photo: 1/20/80; 1/24/82; 2/9/92; 2/22/80; 2/23/85; 3/30/81; 4/21/80; 4/30/93; 9/11/85; 9/29/54; 11/25/80; Adam Butler, 7/8/00, 8/24/04 (Misty May and Kerri Walsh); Al Behrman, 2/27/94, 6/2/85; Amy Sancetta, 3/28/92, 7/23/96; Ben Curtis, 8/24/04 (Yelena Isinbayeva); Bill Haber, 3/30/87; Bill Kostroun, 6/5/04, 7/11/96, 9/21/01, 10/31/01; Bill Waugh, 10/4/89; Bob Dear, 7/4/81; Charles Krupa, 9/5/96, 10/19/04; Chris O'Meara, 1/31/93; Darron Cummings, 5/29/05; Dave Martin, 4/11/04, 4/13/97; David Longstreath, 8/2/92; Denis Paquin, 8/3/92; Donna McWilliam, 3/31/02; Douglas C. Pizac, 11/5/94; Duane Burleson, 11/19/04; Elaine Thompson, 1/25/98, 3/25/06, 5/2/05, 10/8/95; Elise Amendola, 1/19/02, 6/5/02, 10/17/04; Elliot Schecter, 7/4/84, 7/7/01; Eric Gay, 3/21/03, 7/28/94; Eric Jamison, 5/15/04; Eric Risberg, 10/13/01; Eric Sucar, 2/15/06; Frank Franklin II, 7/1/04; Fred Jewell, 10/7/84; Gene Blythe, 4/29/06; Gene Pushkar, 1/11/87; George Widman, 1/16/05; Greg Baker, 7/9/05; Greg Suvino, 2/18/01; Harry Cabluck, 10/21/75, 12/23/73; Jack Smith, 11/5/96, 11/4/97; Jeff Scheid, 2/7/97; Jerry Laizure, 9/26/98; Jim Gerberich, 12/2/87; John Bazemore, 3/23/06; John Gaps III, 1/30/00, 9/8/98; John Swart, 4/1/85, 5/3/86; Jon Freilich, 9/18/99; Joseph Villarin, 6/17/94; Kathy Willens, 9/11/99; Katsumi Kasahara, 9/19/88; Keith Srakocic, 1/14/96; Kevork Djansezian, 10/24/02; Kike del Olmo, 6/30/02; Koji Sasahara, 8/29/04; L.M. Otero, 5/7/95; Laura Rauch, 3/26/05 (Louisville v. W. Virginia); Lennox McLendon, 4/5/84; Lenny Ignelzi, 8/11/05; Leonard Ignelzi, 4/4/83; Linda Kaye, 8/4/93; Lionel Cironneau, 2/16/02; Lou Requena, 5/17/98; Lynne Sladky, 7/29/96; Mark A. Duncan, 9/13/98; Mark Humphrey, 2/5/06; Mark Lennihan, 10/9/96; Matt A. Brown, 1/22/06; Matt Brown, 6/1/04; Michael Conroy, 1/15/06, 3/19/95; Mike Kullen, 4/29/86, 12/12/82; Mike Ridewood, 5/19/84; Molenhouse, 11/21/81; NASCAR, 3/16/03; Paul Vathis, 3/2/62; Phil Sandlin, 4/13/86; Richard Drew, 9/2/91; Rick Bowmer, 2/3/02; Robert Stinnett, 11/20/82; Rodney White, 6/8/96; Ron Edmonds, 9/6/95; Ron Frehm, 10/22/00; Ron Schwane, 7/3/99; Roony Johansson, 8/5/91; Rusty Kennedy, 8/18/01, 10/15/88, 10/25/86; Sadayuki Mikami, 2/11/90; Scott Audette, 8/7/99; Steve Helber, 12/10/04, 3/19/06; Sue Ogrocki, 10/27/04; Susan Ragan, 8/8/92; Ted S. Warren, 1/3/03; Toby Jorrin, 12/28/05; Tom Gannam, 3/5/06; Wade Payne, 1/8/00; Wilfredo Lee, 1/4/05; Winslow Townson, 5/25/02; Winslow Townson, 10/11/03; Bettmann/Corbis: 3/27/83, 4/20/86, 5/16/80, 5/30/82, 10/17/84, 10/12/86, 12/13/83; Bob East III, 1/2/84; Gary Caskey, 8/13/89; Gary Edwards, 2/14/88; Jerry Lodriguss, 3/29/82; Ron Kuntz, 8/10/84; TempSport: 6/4/87; Duomo: Paul J. Sutton, 2/10/02, 6/27/88; Steven E. Sutton, 4/18/83; Getty Images: 3/22/90, 10/14/03, 11/8/99, 11/23/91, 12/1/02 (Michael Vick); Adam Pretty, 8/19/04; AFP, 1/27/95, 2/16/84, 7/23/89; Al Bello, 1/28/96, 3/16/96; Allsport, 8/6/94; Andrew D. Bernstein, 2/6/88, 2/8/86, 5/31/99, 6/20/93; Andrew Redington, 4/10/05; B Bennett, 7/24/83; Bill Baptist, 3/11/04; Billy Stickland, 9/19/00; Bob Martin, 7/2/88; Bongarts, 6/22/86; Brian Bahr, 6/25/98; Bruce Bennett Studios, 2/24/82, 4/6/80, 6/14/94, 8/9/88, 9/15/87, 12/20/83; Clive Brunskill, 2/18/94; Collegiate Images, 3/14/81; Craig Jones, 11/18/96; Darren McNamara, 9/25/00; Dave Cannon, 4/9/89; Dave Rogers, 6/24/95; David Cannon, 8/11/86; David Maxwell, 12/5/04, 12/16/01, 12/27/00; Dirck Halstead, 9/16/81; Don Emmert, 1/23/00; Doug Benc, 10/9/05; Doug Pensinger, 1/11/04, 8/30/97;

Elsa Hasch, 5/31/97; Ezra Shaw, 10/3/99; Fernando Medina, 5/16/99; Focus on Sport, 5/20/89, 9/4/93; Gary Newkirk, 2/27/92; Gunnar Berning, 8/1/96; Harry How, 1/4/06; Henny Ray Abrams, 5/14/96; Henri Szwarc, 7/17/94; Javier Soriano, 8/27/04; Jed Jacobsohn, 6/28/97, 12/22/03; Jeff Gross, 3/22/03; Jim Bourg, 9/26/99; Joe Klamar, 2/17/06; Joel Saget, 7/17/01; John G. Mabanglo, 10/5/01; Jonathan Daniel, 3/26/05 (Illinois v. Arizona), 4/8/96, 8/8/88, 10/15/05, 11/22/97, 12/2/85; Kim Jae-Hwan, 9/27/00; Matt Rourke, 5/22/03; Mike Nelson, 11/4/01; Mike Powell, 2/12/06; Nathaniel S. Butler, 4/16/96, 5/25/93, 6/4/03, 6/7/95; National Baseball Hall of Fame Library, 5/1/91; Nick Laham, 5/7/05; Omar Torres, 6/29/94, 7/19/96; Otto Greule, 12/6/92; Paul Spinelli, 11/15/04; Peter Muhly, 11/24/02; Rick Stewart, 1/3/93, 10/23/93; Robert Laberge, 2/11/02; Rob Taggart, 7/5/80; Roberto Schmidt, 7/10/99; Ross Kinnaird; 6/30/98; Scott Cunningham, 6/14/98; Scott Halleran, 11/26/94; Stephen Dunn, 10/21/04; Stephen Munday, 4/14/96; Tom Hauck, 11/14/98; Trevor Jones, 8/3/84; Victor Baldizon, 11/7/05, 11/18/05; William Snyder, 11/29/97; Phil Sheldon Golf Picture Library, 7/19/92; Reuters Pictures: 2/15/98; Adrees Latif, 7/10/01; Charles Platiau, 7/12/98; Ian Waldie, 6/29/01; Jeff J. Mitchell, 7/18/99; Lucy Nicholson, 12/3/05 (Reggie Bush); Mark Baker, 1/21/90; Peter Schols, 7/9/06; Ray Stubblebine, 6/12/01, 6/15/02, 10/23/00; Scott Olson, 8/15/99; Tim Shaffer, 4/19/05; Seattle Times: Harley Soltes, 1/1/85; Sports Illustrated Pictures: Bob Rosato, 9/22/02; John Biever, 3/29/03; John Iacono, 12/11/81; Manny Millan, 4/4/88, 4/17/87; Neil Leifer, 2/25/64, 9/29/88; Richard Mackson, 1/17/88, 6/20/82; Tony Triolo, 4/8/74; Walter Iooss Jr., 1/10/82; V.J. Lovero, 10/27/91; Sports Action: Brian Babineau, 4/10/04; Sports Chrome: 1/26/86; Rob Tringali, 3/10/06; St. Paul Star Tribune: Brian Peterson, 5/10/03; Toronto Star: Dick Loek, 8/4/89; Richard Lautens, 10/20/92. **Video Credits** Courtesy of ESPN Enterprises, Inc.: 1/29/05, 2/6/82, 5/24/03, 6/27/99, 8/5/04, 8/16/02, 8/16/03, 8/17/02; Courtesy of Intersport, Inc: 1/6/94; Courtesy of KOIN TV Portland: 5/27/91; Courtesy of Loews Motor Speedway: 5/17/87, 5/21/89; Courtesy of Major League Baseball: 3/24/01, 4/19/00, 4/22/96, 4/26/89, 5/4/84, 5/5/93, 5/11/06, 5/26/93, 5/27/81, 6/9/99, 6/15/91, 7/6/02, 7/8/94, 7/16/90, 7/25/92, 8/7/02, 8/21/90, 9/7/93, 9/14/90, 9/17/02, 9/28/05; 10/26/85; Courtesy of Motorsports Images & Archives Photography. Used with permission: 8/31/97; Courtesy of the National Basketball Association: 2/26/96, 5/5/81, 5/28/00, 12/17/91, 12/27/91; Courtesy of the National Football League: 9/12/82, 9/30/02, 10/6/02, 11/21/99, 11/26/89, 11/28/04, 12/1/02 (Bears vs. Packers), 12/9/01 (Jeff Graham), 12/18/05, 12/21/03, 12/25/04; Courtesy of the National Hockey League: 1/16/06, 4/14/91, 10/18/02, 12/8/87, 12/9/01 (Craig Johnson); Courtesy of PGA Tour: 3/1/91; Courtesy of Thought Equity and Collegiate Images: 1/25/88, 9/24/94, 11/8/97, 11/13/93, 11/17/01, 11/23/84, 12/3/05 (Northwest Missouri State vs. North Alabama), 12/4/88, 12/22/84; Courtesy of Thought Equity and Lincoln Financial Sports: 9/10/05, 9/14/02, 10/8/88, 11/9/02, 11/30/85; Courtesy of Thought Equity and the NCAA: 3/13/98, 3/14/96, 3/18/99, 3/20/81, 3/20/94, 3/24/96, 4/1/91, 4/5/93, 12/11/99; Courtesy of Thought Equity and Raycom Sports: 2/2/95, 11/2/95, 11/3/90, 11/10/84, 11/16/91, 12/15/02, 12/23/82; Courtesy of the U.S. Olympic Committee: 2/13/98, 7/29/92; Courtesy of the United States Basketball League: 6/10/86; Courtesy of the USGA Archives: 6/17/84; Courtesy of Viacom, Inc.: 6/19/00

ESPN Books are available for special promotions and premiums. For details contact Michael Rentas, Assistant Director, Inventory Operations, Hyperion, 77 West 66th Street, 11th floor, New York, New York 10023, or call 212-456-0133

ISBN-10: 1-933060-21-2
ISBN-13: 978-1-933060-21-7

First Hardcover Edition
October 2006

10 9 8 7 6 5 4 3 2 1

a division of

ESPN publishing

Acknowledgments:

Thanks to Kyle Acebo, Donna Aceto, Jonathan Ambar, Peter Andrus, Cathy Beazley, Chris Berman, Jason Catania, Mike Cocchi, Michael Corcoran, Charles Curtis, Max Dickstein, Chris Dolin, John Hassan, Paul Lukas, David McAninch, Doug Mittler, Lauren Nathan, Julia Neilson, Kenneth Partridge, Michael Pierce, Lia Ronnen, Holly Rothman, Jessi Rymill, Alex Tart, Shoshana Thaler, Jared Ward, Carl Williamson, Craig Winston, Betty Wong, and Megan Worman

This book was produced by

124 West 13th Street
New York, New York 10011
www.melcher.com

Publisher: Charles Melcher
Associate Publisher: Bonnie Eldon
Editor in Chief: Duncan Bock
Editor: David E. Brown
Assistant Editor: Lindsey Stanberry
Production Director: Andrea Hirsh

Book design: Plazm / Joshua Berger, Todd Houlette
www.plazm.com